THE NEW FOLGER LIBRARY SHAKESPEARE

Designed to make Shakespeare's great plays available to all readers, the New Folger Library edition of Shakespeare's plays provides accurate texts in modern spelling and punctuation, as well as scene-by-scene action summaries, full explanatory notes, many pictures clarifying Shakespeare's language, and notes recording all significant departures from the early printed versions. Each play is prefaced by a brief introduction, by a guide to reading Shakespeare's language, and by accounts of his life and theater. Each play is followed by an annotated list of further readings and by a "Modern Perspective" written by an expert on that particular play.

Barbara A. Mowat is Director of Research *emerita* at the Folger Shakespeare Library, Consulting Editor of *Shakespeare Quarterly*, and author of *The Dramaturgy of Shakespeare's Romances* and of essays on Shakespeare's plays and their editing.

Paul Werstine is Professor of English in the Graduate School and at King's University College at Western University. He is a general editor of the New Variorum Shakespeare and author of *Early Modern Playhouse Manuscripts and the Editing of Shakespeare*, as well as many papers and essays on the printing and editing of Shakespeare's plays.

Folger Shakespeare Library

The Folger Shakespeare Library in Washington, D.C., is a privately funded research library dedicated to Shakespeare and the civilization of early modern Europe. It was founded in 1932 by Henry Clay and Emily Jordan Folger, and incorporated as part of Amherst College in Amherst, Massachusetts, one of the nation's oldest liberal arts colleges, from which Henry Folger had graduated in 1879. In addition to its role as the world's preeminent Shakespeare collection and its emergence as a leading center for Renaissance studies, the Folger Shakespeare Library offers a wide array of cultural and educational programs and services for the general public.

EDITORS

BARBARA A. MOWAT
Director of Research emerita
Folger Shakespeare Library

PAUL WERSTINE
Professor of English
King's University College at the
University of Western Ontario, Canada

The Tempest

By
WILLIAM SHAKESPEARE

An Updated Edition

Edited by Barbara A. Mowat
and Paul Werstine

Simon & Schuster Paperbacks
New York London Toronto Sydney New Delhi

Simon & Schuster Paperbacks
A Division of Simon & Schuster, Inc.
1230 Avenue of the Americas
New York, NY 10020

Washington Square Press New Folger Edition May 1994
This Simon & Schuster paperback edition January 2016

SIMON & SCHUSTER PAPERBACKS and colophon are registered trademarks of Simon & Schuster, Inc.

For information regarding special discounts for bulk purchases, please contact Simon & Schuster Special Sales at 1-866-506-1949 or business@simonandschuster.com.

The Simon & Schuster Speakers Bureau can bring authors to your live event. For more information or to book an event, contact the Simon & Schuster Speakers Bureau at 1-866-248-3049 or visit our website at www.simonspeakers.com.

Manufactured in the United States of America

30   29   28   27

ISBN 978-0-7434-8283-7
ISBN 978-1-4767-8859-3 (ebook)

From the Director of the Folger Shakespeare Library

It is hard to imagine a world without Shakespeare. Since their composition four hundred years ago, Shakespeare's plays and poems have traveled the globe, inviting those who see and read his works to make them their own.

Readers of the New Folger Editions are part of this ongoing process of "taking up Shakespeare," finding our own thoughts and feelings in language that strikes us as old or unusual and, for that very reason, new. We still struggle to keep up with a writer who could think a mile a minute, whose words paint pictures that shift like clouds. These expertly edited texts, presented here with accompanying explanatory notes and up-to-date critical essays, are distinctive because of what they do: they allow readers not simply to keep up, but to engage deeply with a writer whose works invite us to think, and think again.

These New Folger Editions of Shakespeare's plays are also special because of where they come from. The Folger Shakespeare Library in Washington, DC, where the Editions are produced, is the single greatest documentary source of Shakespeare's works. An unparalleled collection of early modern books, manuscripts, and artwork connected to Shakespeare, the Folger's holdings have been consulted extensively in the preparation of these texts. The Editions also reflect the expertise gained through the regular performance of Shakespeare's works in the Folger's Elizabethan Theater.

I want to express my deep thanks to editors Barbara Mowat and Paul Werstine for creating these indispensable editions of Shakespeare's works, which incorporate the best of textual scholarship with a richness of commentary that is both inspired and engaging. Readers who want to know more about Shakespeare and his plays can follow the paths these distinguished scholars have tread by visiting the Folger itself, where a range of physical and digital resources (available online) exist to supplement the material in these texts. I commend to you these words, and hope that they inspire.

Michael Witmore
Director, Folger Shakespeare Library

Contents

Editors' Preface

In recent years, ways of dealing with Shakespeare's texts and with the interpretation of his plays have been undergoing significant change. This edition, while retaining many of the features that have always made the Folger Shakespeare so attractive to the general reader, at the same time reflects these current ways of thinking about Shakespeare. For example, modern readers, actors, and teachers have become interested in the differences between, on the one hand, the early forms in which Shakespeare's plays were first published and, on the other hand, the forms in which editors through the centuries have presented them. In response to this interest, we have based our edition on what we consider the best early printed version of a particular play (explaining our rationale in a section called "An Introduction to This Text") and have marked our changes in the text—unobtrusively, we hope, but in such a way that the curious reader can be aware that a change has been made and can consult the "Textual Notes" to discover what appeared in the early printed version.

Current ways of looking at the plays are reflected in our brief introductions, in many of the commentary notes, in the annotated lists of "Further Reading," and especially in each play's "Modern Perspective," an essay written by an outstanding scholar who brings to the reader his or her fresh assessment of the play in the light of today's interests and concerns.

As in the Folger Library General Reader's Shakespeare, which the New Folger Library Shakespeare replaces, we include explanatory notes designed to help make Shakespeare's language clearer to a modern reader, and we place the notes on the page facing the text that they explain. We also follow the earlier edition in including illustrations—of objects, of clothing, of mythological figures—from books and manuscripts in the Folger Library collection. We provide fresh accounts of the life of Shakespeare, of the publishing of his plays, and of the theaters in which his plays were performed, as well as an introduction to the text itself. We also include a section called "Reading Shakespeare's Language," in which we try to help readers learn to "break the code" of Elizabethan poetic language.

For each section of each volume, we are indebted to a host of generous experts and fellow scholars. The "Reading Shakespeare's Language" sections, for example, could not have been written had not Arthur King, of Brigham Young University, and Randal Robinson, author of *Unlocking Shakespeare's Language*, led the way in untangling Shakespearean language puzzles and generously shared their insights and methodologies with us. "Shakespeare's Life" profited by the careful reading given it by S. Schoenbaum; "Shakespeare's Theater" was read and strengthened by Andrew Gurr, John Astington, and William Ingram. "The Publication of Shakespeare's Plays" is indebted to the comments of Peter W. M. Blayney. We, as editors, take sole responsibility for any errors in our editions.

We are grateful to the authors of the "Modern Perspectives"; to Leeds Barroll and David Bevington for their generous encouragement; to the Huntington and Newberry Libraries for fellowship support; to King's University College for the grants it has provided to Paul Werstine; to the Social Sciences and Humanities Research Council of Canada, which provided him with Research Time Stipends; to R. J. Shroyer of Western University for essential computer support; and to the

Folger Institute's Center for Shakespeare Studies for its fortuitous sponsorship of a workshop on "Shakespeare's Texts for Students and Teachers" (funded by the National Endowment for the Humanities and led by Richard Knowles of the University of Wisconsin), a workshop from which we learned an enormous amount about what is wanted by college and high-school teachers of Shakespeare today.

In preparing this preface for the publication of *The Tempest* in 1994, we wrote: "Our biggest debt is to the Folger Shakespeare Library—to Werner Gundersheimer, Director of the Library, who made possible our edition; to Jean Miller, the Library's Art Curator, who combs the library holdings for illustrations, and to Julie Ainsworth, Head of the Photography Department, who carefully photographs them; to Peggy O'Brien, Director of Education, and her assistant, Molly Haws, who continue to give us expert advice about the needs being expressed by Shakespeare teachers and students (and to Martha Christian and other "master teachers" who used our texts in manuscript in their classrooms); to Jessica Hymowitz, who provides expert computer support; to the staff of the Academic Programs Division, especially Mary Tonkinson, Lena Cowen Orlin, Jean Feerick, Amy Adler, Kathleen Lynch, and Carol Brobeck; and, finally, to the staff of the Library Reading Room, whose patience and support are invaluable."

As we revise the play for publication in 2015, we add to the above our gratitude to Michael Witmore, Director of the Folger Shakespeare Library, who brings to our work a gratifying enthusiasm and vision; to Gail Kern Paster, Director of the Library from 2002 until July 2011, whose interest and support have been unfailing and whose scholarly expertise continues to be an invaluable resource; to Jonathan Evans and Alysha Bullock, our production editors at Simon & Schuster, whose expertise, attention to detail, and wisdom are essential to this project; to the Folger's Photography Department; to Deborah Curren-Aquino for continuing superb editorial assistance; to Alice Falk for her expert copyediting; to Michael Poston for unfailing computer support; to Anna Levine; and to Rebecca Niles (whose help is crucial). Among the editions we consulted, we found Virginia and Alden Vaughan's 1999 Arden edition especially useful. Finally, we once again express our thanks to Stephen Llano for twenty-five years of support as our invaluable production editor, to the late Jean Miller for the wonderful images she unearthed, and to the ever-supportive staff of the Library Reading Room.

Barbara A. Mowat and Paul Werstine
2015

Shakespeare's *The Tempest*

In *The Tempest* Shakespeare puts romance onstage. He gives us a magician, a monster, a grief-stricken king, a wise old councillor, and no fewer than two beautiful princesses (one of whom we only hear about) and two treacherous brothers. The magician is Prospero, former duke of the Italian city-state of Milan, whose intense attraction to the study of magic caused him to lose sight of the political necessity of maintaining power, which he then lost to his treacherous brother, Antonio. When we first meet Prospero, he has already suffered twelve years of exile on a desert island, where his only companions have been his daughter, Miranda, now a beautiful princess; the spirit Ariel; and the monster Caliban, whom Prospero has used his magic to enslave. Now, sailing by the island and caught in a terrible storm are Prospero's enemies (and one of his friends), who are returning from North Africa after having attended the wedding of another beautiful princess, Claribel of Naples, and the king of Tunis. On the ship are Antonio, who usurped Prospero's dukedom and put him out to sea; King Alonso of Naples, who conspired with Antonio against Prospero; Sebastian, Alonso's brother, who is about to conspire with Antonio against Alonso; Prince Ferdinand, Alonso's son, destined to discover and fall into the power of the beautiful Miranda; and finally, Gonzalo, the wise old councillor who, twelve years before, provided Prospero with the books and other necessities that have made it possible for Prospero not only to survive his exile but also to grow ever more powerful as a magician. Prospero will now turn his awesome power upon his enemies through the agency of Ariel (and the many

"If by your art . . . you have / Put the wild waters
in this roar." (1.2.1–2)
From Guillaume de la Perrière, *La morosophie* . . . (1553).

other spirits whom Ariel directs) in producing terror in Prospero's victims and pleasure in those whom Prospero favors.

Yet *The Tempest* is more than romance, for its characters exceed the roles of villains and heroes, some of them becoming both villains and heroes. Prospero seems heroic in enduring his long exile, in protecting his daughter from Caliban, and in mastering a spirit world that he can use to control the elements and much else, but he also seems villainous in his enslavement of others, notably Caliban, and his enormous appetite for revenge on his enemies. Caliban seems to deserve the name of monster for his attack upon Miranda, but he also seems heroic in his resistance to Prospero, who wrests the island from him and attempts to tyrannize over him. Thus *The Tempest* belongs not only to the world of romance but also to the period of colonialism, written as it was in the very early stages of the European exploration and conquest of the New World.

The doubleness that we see in the play's embodiment of seemingly timeless romance and a temporally specific historical moment is characteristic of this complex play, which seems simple and lyrical but which contains wonderfully complex narratives and emotions. For an examination of these complexities, we invite you to turn, after you have read the play, to the essay printed after it titled "*The Tempest:* A Modern Perspective," written by Barbara A. Mowat.

Reading Shakespeare's Language:
The Tempest

For many people today, reading Shakespeare's language can be a problem—but it is a problem that can be solved. Those who have studied Latin (or even French or German or Spanish) and those who are used to reading poetry will have little difficulty understanding the language of Shakespeare's poetic drama. Others, however, need to develop the skills of untangling unusual sentence structures and of recognizing and understanding poetic compressions, omissions, and wordplay. And even those skilled in reading unusual sentence structures may have occasional trouble with Shakespeare's words. More than four hundred years of "static"—caused by changes in language and life—intervene between his speaking and our hearing. Most of his immense vocabulary is still in use, but a few of his words are no longer used, and many of his words now have meanings quite different from those they had in the seventeenth century. In the theater, most of these difficulties are solved for us by actors who study the language and articulate it for us so that the essential meaning is heard—or, when combined with stage action, is at least *felt*. When reading on one's own, one must do what each actor does: go over the lines (often with a dictionary close at hand) until the puzzles are solved and the lines yield up their poetry and the characters speak in words and phrases that are, suddenly, rewarding and wonderfully memorable.

Shakespeare's Words

As you begin to read the opening scenes of a Shakespeare play, you may notice occasional unfamiliar words. Some are unfamiliar simply because we no longer use them. In the opening scenes of *The Tempest*, for example, you will find the words *yarely* (i.e., quickly, nimbly), *hap* (i.e., happen), *fain* (i.e., gladly), *wrack* (i.e., wrecked vessel), and *teen* (i.e., trouble). Words of this kind are explained in notes to the text and will become familiar the more of Shakespeare's plays you read.

In *The Tempest*, as in all of Shakespeare's writing, more problematic are the words that are still in use but that now have different meanings. In the opening scenes of *The Tempest*, for example, the word *hearts* has the meaning of "hearties, good fellows," *hand* is used where we would say "handle, lay hold of," *art* is used where we would say "learning" or "skill," *brave* where we would say "splendid," and *perdition* where we would say "loss." Again, such words will be explained in the notes to the text, but they, too, will become familiar as you continue to read Shakespeare's language.

Some words are strange not because of the "static" introduced by changes in language over the past centuries but because these are words that Shakespeare uses to build a dramatic world that has its own space, time, and history. In the opening scenes of *The Tempest*, for example, Shakespeare quickly creates the world of the storm-tossed ship, with words like "boatswain" and with such nautical terminology as "bring her to try wi' th' main course," "lay her ahold," and "set her two courses." He then builds the island world in which Prospero and Miranda presently live, a world dominated by Prospero's "art" (i.e., his magic power), a world where

Prospero is master of a "full poor cell," where he "sties" Caliban in a "rock," a world of "urchins" and "marmosets" and "pignuts." Simultaneously, Shakespeare creates the world of Prospero and Miranda's past, a world of "signiories," "coronets," and "tribute," of "the liberal arts" and "secret studies," of confederacy and extirpation. Ariel enters, bringing with him the language of service: "grave sir," "hests," "task" (i.e., put to work), "bad'st" (i.e., commanded); Caliban brings his curses. As each new character enters, he brings a few linguistic signs of his past and his character. The language world of this play thus builds gradually and cumulatively, in contrast to most of Shakespeare's plays where the dimensions of a particular world are clearly laid out in the first two or three scenes.

Shakespeare's Sentences

In an English sentence, meaning is quite dependent on the place given each word. "The dog bit the boy" and "The boy bit the dog" mean very different things, even though the individual words are the same. Because English places such importance on the positions of words in sentences, on the way words are arranged, unusual arrangements can puzzle a reader. Shakespeare frequently shifts his sentences away from "normal" English arrangements—often in order to create the rhythm he seeks, sometimes in order to use a line's poetic rhythm to emphasize a particular word, sometimes to give a character his or her own speech patterns or to allow the character to speak in a special way. When we attend a good performance of a play, the actors will have worked out the sentence structures and will articulate the sentences so that the meaning is clear. When reading the play, we need to do as the actor does: that is, when puzzled by a character's speech, check to see if words are being presented in an unusual sequence.

Shakespeare often rearranges subjects and verbs (e.g., instead of "He goes" we find "Goes he," or instead of "I would go" we find "Would I go"). In *The Tempest*, when Gonzalo says "Now *would I give* a thousand furlongs of sea" (1.1.68), he is using such a construction. Shakespeare also frequently places the object or the predicate adjective or predicate nominative before the subject and verb (e.g., instead of "I hit him," we might find "Him I hit," or, instead of "It is black," we might find "Black it is"). Prospero's "The *government I cast* upon my brother" (1.2.93) is an example of such an inversion, as is his "*a cherubin / Thou wast* that did preserve me" (1.2.182–83). Ferdinand, too, uses such a construction in his "*Space enough / Have I* in such a prison" (1.2.599–600), which also inverts the subject and verb. The "normal" order would be "I have space enough. . . ."

Often in *The Tempest* Shakespeare uses inverted sentences that fall outside even these categories. Such sentences must be studied individually until the "normal" sentence pattern can be perceived. Prospero's "By foul play, as thou sayst, were we heaved thence" (1.2.78) is a relatively simple example of such an inversion. Its "normal" order would be "As thou sayst, we were heaved thence by foul play." Miranda's "More to know / Did never meddle with my thoughts" (1.2.25–26) is more complicated. Its "normal" order would be, approximately, "To know more never did meddle. . . ."

Inversions are not the only unusual sentence structures in Shakespeare's language. Often in his sentences words that would normally appear together are separated from each other. (Again, this is often done to create a particular rhythm or to stress a particular word.) Take, for example, Prospero's "*The direful spectacle* of the wrack, which touched / The very virtue of compassion in thee, / *I have* with such provision in mine art / So safely *ordered* . . ." (1.2.33–36). Here, the phrase "with such provision in mine art so safely" separates the parts of the verb "have ordered," while several phrases and a clause separate the subject and verb from the object ("The direful spectacle"); since the object stands first, the sentence also inverts the "normal" order of subject-verb-object. Or take Ferdinand's lines "*I*, / Beyond all limit of what else i' th' world, / *Do love, prize, honor you*" (3.1.84–86). Here, the subject and verb "I do love, prize, honor" are interrupted by the insertion of the phrase "Beyond all limit of what else i' th' world." In order to create sentences that seem more like the English of everyday speech, you can rearrange the words, putting together the word clusters ("I have so safely ordered the direful spectacle . . . ," "I do love, prize, honor . . ."). The result will usually be an increase in clarity but a loss of rhythm or a shift in emphasis.

Locating and if necessary rearranging words that "belong together" is especially helpful in passages with long delaying or expanding interruptions. When Prospero tells Miranda about his former seclusion and its effect on his brother ("I awaked an evil nature in my false brother"), he uses such an interrupted construction:

> *I*, thus neglecting worldly ends, all dedicated
> To closeness and the bettering of my mind
> With that which, but by being so retired,
> O'erprized all popular rate, *in my false brother*
> *Awaked an evil nature*. . . .   (1.2.109–13)

Shakespeare's sentences are sometimes complicated not because of unusual structures or interruptions or delays but because he omits words and parts of words that English sentences normally require. (In conversation, we, too, often omit words. We say "Heard from him yet?" and our hearer supplies the missing "Have you.") Frequent reading of Shakespeare—and of other poets—trains us to supply such missing words. In his later plays, including *The Tempest*, Shakespeare uses omissions of words to great dramatic effect. Ferdinand's "Vouchsafe my prayer / May know if you remain upon this island" (1.2.506–7) compresses the request "Vouchsafe [to hear] my prayer [that I] may know if you remain upon this island." The compressed statement (in which the prayer itself is "vouchsafed" and is also given the capacity to "know") conveys both the power of the emotion that seizes Ferdinand and the formality appropriate for an address to a goddess. Ferdinand's "He does hear me, / And that he does I weep. Myself am Naples" (1.2.520–21) compresses "He does hear me, and [it is because he does that] I weep. [I] myself am Naples." The heavily compressed statement both expresses Ferdinand's grief and reflects what he thinks is his new status as king (*"Myself* am Naples"). His exclamation to Miranda, "O, if a virgin, / And your affection not gone forth" (1.2.538–39), compresses "O, if [you are] a virgin, / And [if] your affection [has] not gone forth." The compression conveys Ferdinand's desire and his anxiety that Miranda might already be committed to someone else. When he later commits himself to her, his language is so compressed that one cannot be certain of its exact meaning; only the intensity of feeling comes through: "My husband, then?" "Ay, with a heart as willing / As bondage e'er of freedom" (3.1.105–7). We have, in our gloss to these lines, suggested that "as bondage e'er of freedom" might mean "as the enslaved ever wished for liberty"—an attempt at rephrasing that, in its inadequacy, simply points up the power of the words given Ferdinand to speak.

Shakespearean Wordplay

Shakespeare plays with language so often and so variously that entire books are written on the topic. Here we will mention only two kinds of wordplay, puns and metaphors. A pun is a play on words that sound the same but that have different meanings (or on a single word that has more than one meaning). In *The Tempest*, two sets of characters use puns. Antonio and Sebastian use them to mock other people. When, at 2.1.18–19, Gonzalo says "When every grief is entertained [i.e., received] that's offered, comes to th' entertainer [i.e., the one who accepts (the grief)]," Sebastian interrupts him with the words "A dollar" (line 20), indirectly punning on "entertainer" as meaning one who amuses others and gets paid for it. Gonzalo responds with a pun of his own, saying that "Dolor [i.e., sorrow] comes to him indeed" (line 21). When Gonzalo says, at 2.1.61–62, "But the rarity [i.e., exceptional quality] of it is, which is indeed almost beyond credit [i.e., belief]," Sebastian again interrupts, saying "As many vouched rarities are" (line 63), punning on "rarity" as an unusual occurrence or freak of nature.

Stephano and Trinculo also pun, but they do so to amuse themselves and each other. At 3.2.16–19, when Stephano says to Caliban "Thou shalt be my lieutenant, monster, or my standard [i.e., standard-bearer or ensign]," Trinculo responds with "Your lieutenant, if you list [i.e., please]. He's no standard," punning on "standard" as an upright timber or pole and calling attention to how falling-down drunk Caliban is. At 3.2.35–36, Trinculo's comment about Caliban, "That a monster should be such a natural!" plays with two meanings of the word "natural," saying that Caliban, though a monster (and hence unnatural), is a simpleton or idiot (i.e., a natural). Although large sections of *The Tempest* contain no puns, language in the scenes with Sebastian and Antonio and those with Stephano and Trinculo needs to be listened to especially carefully if one is to catch all its meanings.

A metaphor is a play on words in which one object or idea is expressed as if it were something else, something with which it is said to share common features. For instance, when Prospero asks Miranda "What seest thou else / In the dark backward and abysm of time?" (1.2.61–62), he is using metaphorical language to describe the past as if it were a dark abyss. When he describes his treacherous brother as "The ivy which had hid my princely trunk / And sucked my verdure out on 't" (1.2.105–6), he again uses a metaphor; here, Prospero is a tree and Antonio is parasitical ivy. Alonso uses metaphorical language when he says, in response to the Harpy's speech, "The winds did sing it to me, and the thunder, / That deep and dreadful organ pipe, pronounced / The name of Prosper. It did bass my trespass" (3.3.118–20). The speech of accusation, he says, has come to his ears like the sound of thunder; the power of the metaphor is heightened by the wordplay on "did bass my trespass," which can mean (1) provided a bass accompaniment to the singing of the wind; (2) intoned my sin in bass notes; and (3) proclaimed the baseness of my actions. Metaphors are often used when the idea being conveyed is hard to express, or, as is often the case in *The Tempest*, used as a kind of shorthand to convey an idea and its attendant emotions swiftly to the speaker's listener—and to the audience.

Implied Stage Action

Finally, in reading Shakespeare's plays we should always remember that what we are reading is a performance script. The dialogue is written to be spoken by actors who, at the same time, are moving, gesturing, picking up objects, weeping, shaking their fists. Some stage action is described in what are called "stage directions"; some is suggested within the dialogue itself. We must learn to be alert to such signals as we stage the play in our imaginations. When, in *The Tempest* 1.2.28–31, Prospero says to Miranda "Lend thy hand / And pluck my magic garment from me," and then says immediately "So, / Lie there, my art [i.e., my magic power]," it is clear that Prospero's cloak is removed and placed somewhere on the stage. When, at 1.2.363–66, Prospero says to Miranda "Awake, dear heart, awake. Thou hast slept well. / Awake," and Miranda responds "The strangeness of your story put / Heaviness [i.e., sleepiness] in me," it is equally clear that Miranda has been lying down and now rouses up.

Occasionally in *The Tempest*, signals to the reader are not quite so clear. In the final scene of the play, for example, Ferdinand and Miranda are "discovered" sitting and playing a game of chess (5.1.199 SD). Ferdinand sees his lost father, stands, and comes forward, saying "Though the seas threaten, they are merciful. / I have cursed them without cause," and Alonso responds "Now, all the blessings / Of a glad father compass thee about! / Arise, and say how thou cam'st here" (lines 209–14). Alonso's "Arise" lets us know that Ferdinand at some point in this exchange has kneeled; it is not clear, however, at which moment he kneels, nor is it certain when he again stands. Nor is it clear when Miranda rises and comes forward to say "O, brave new world . . ." (line 217). We as editors have inserted stage directions at what seemed to us the most probable places, but these are ultimately matters that directors and actors—and readers in their imaginations—must decide. Learning to read the language of stage action repays one many times over when one reaches a crucial scene like that of the Harpy/king confrontation in 3.3 or that of the presentation of the masque in 4.1, in both of which scenes implied stage action vitally affects our response to the play.

It is immensely rewarding to work carefully with Shakespeare's language—with the words, the sentences, the wordplay, and the implied stage action—as readers for the past four centuries have discovered. It may be more pleasurable to attend a good performance of a play—though not everyone has thought so. But the joy of being able to stage one of Shakespeare's plays in one's imagination, to return to passages that continue to yield further meanings (or further questions) the more one reads them—these are pleasures that, for many, rival (or at least augment) those of the performed text, and certainly make it worth considerable effort to "break the code" of Elizabethan poetic drama and let free the remarkable language that makes up a Shakespeare text.

Shakespeare's Life

Surviving documents that give us glimpses into the life of William Shakespeare show us a playwright, poet, and actor who grew up in the market town of Stratford-upon-Avon, spent his professional life in London, and returned to Stratford a wealthy landowner. He was born in April 1564, died in April 1616, and is buried inside the chancel of Holy Trinity Church in Stratford.

We wish we could know more about the life of the world's greatest dramatist. His plays and poems are testaments to his wide reading—especially to his knowledge of Virgil, Ovid, Plutarch, Holinshed's *Chronicles*, and the Bible—and to his mastery of the English language, but we can only speculate about his education. We know that the King's New School in Stratford-upon-Avon was considered excellent. The school was one of the English "grammar schools" established to educate young men, primarily in Latin grammar and literature. As in other schools of the time, students began their studies at the age of four or five in the attached "petty school," and there learned to read and write in English, studying primarily the catechism from the Book of Common Prayer. After two years in the petty school, students entered the lower form (grade) of the grammar school, where they began the serious study of Latin grammar and Latin texts that would occupy most of the remainder of their school days. (Several Latin texts that Shakespeare used repeatedly in writing his plays and poems were texts that schoolboys memorized and recited.) Latin comedies were introduced early in the lower form; in the upper form, which the boys entered at age ten or eleven, students wrote their own Latin orations and declamations, studied Latin historians and rhetoricians, and began the study of Greek using the Greek New Testament.

Since the records of the Stratford "grammar school" do not survive, we cannot prove that William Shakespeare attended the school; however, every indication (his father's position as an alderman and bailiff of Stratford, the playwright's own knowledge of the Latin classics, scenes in the plays that recall grammar-school experiences—for example, *The Merry Wives of Wind-*

Title page of a 1573 Latin and Greek catechism for children.
From Alexander Nowell, *Catechismus paruus pueris
primum Latine . . .* (1573).

sor, 4.1) suggests that he did. We also lack generally accepted documentation about Shakespeare's life after his schooling ended and his professional life in London began. His marriage in 1582 (at age eighteen) to Anne Hathaway and the subsequent births of his daughter Susanna (1583) and the twins Judith and Hamnet (1585) are recorded, but how he supported himself and where he lived are not known. Nor do we know when and why he left Stratford for the London theatrical world, nor how he rose to be the important figure in that world that he had become by the early 1590s.

We do know that by 1592 he had achieved some prominence in London as both an actor and a playwright. In that year was published a book by the playwright Robert Greene attacking an actor who had the audacity to write blank-verse drama and who was "in his own conceit [i.e., opinion] the only Shake-scene in a country." Since Greene's attack includes a parody of a line from one of Shakespeare's early plays, there is little doubt that it is Shakespeare to whom he refers, a "Shake-scene" who had aroused Greene's fury by successfully competing with university-educated dramatists like Greene himself. It was in 1593 that Shakespeare became a published poet. In that year he published his long narrative poem *Venus and Adonis*; in 1594, he followed it with *The Rape of Lucrece*. Both poems were dedicated to the young earl of Southampton (Henry Wriothesley), who may have become Shakespeare's patron.

It seems no coincidence that Shakespeare wrote these narrative poems at a time when the theaters were closed because of the plague, a contagious epidemic disease that devastated the population of London. When the theaters reopened in 1594, Shakespeare apparently resumed his double career of actor and playwright and began his long (and seemingly profitable) service as an

acting-company shareholder. Records for December of
1594 show him to be a leading member of the Lord
Chamberlain's Men. It was this company of actors,
later named the King's Men, for whom he would be a
principal actor, dramatist, and shareholder for the rest
of his career.

So far as we can tell, that career spanned about
twenty years. In the 1590s, he wrote his plays on
English history as well as several comedies and at least
two tragedies (*Titus Andronicus* and *Romeo and Juliet*).
These histories, comedies, and tragedies are the plays
credited to him in 1598 in a work, *Palladis Tamia*, that
in one chapter compares English writers with "Greek,
Latin, and Italian Poets." There the author, Francis
Meres, claims that Shakespeare is comparable to the
Latin dramatists Seneca for tragedy and Plautus for
comedy, and calls him "the most excellent in both kinds
for the stage." He also names him "Mellifluous and
honey-tongued Shakespeare": "I say," writes Meres,
"that the Muses would speak with Shakespeare's fine
filed phrase, if they would speak English." Since Meres
also mentions Shakespeare's "sugared sonnets among
his private friends," it is assumed that many of Shakespeare's sonnets (not published until 1609) were also
written in the 1590s.

In 1599, Shakespeare's company built a theater
for themselves across the river from London, naming
it the Globe. The plays that are considered by many
to be Shakespeare's major tragedies (*Hamlet, Othello,
King Lear,* and *Macbeth*) were written while the company was resident in this theater, as were such comedies as *Twelfth Night* and *Measure for Measure.* Many
of Shakespeare's plays were performed at court (both
for Queen Elizabeth I and, after her death in 1603,
for King James I), some were presented at the Inns
of Court (the residences of London's legal societies),

and some were doubtless performed in other towns, at the universities, and at great houses when the King's Men went on tour; otherwise, his plays from 1599 to 1608 were, so far as we know, performed only at the Globe. Between 1608 and 1612, Shakespeare wrote several plays—among them *The Winter's Tale* and *The Tempest*—presumably for the company's new indoor Blackfriars theater, though the plays were performed also at the Globe and at court. Surviving documents describe a performance of *The Winter's Tale* in 1611 at the Globe, for example, and performances of *The Tempest* in 1611 and 1613 at the royal palace of Whitehall.

Shakespeare seems to have written very little after 1612, the year in which he probably wrote *King Henry VIII*. (It was at a performance of *Henry VIII* in 1613 that the Globe caught fire and burned to the ground.) Sometime between 1610 and 1613, according to many biographers, he returned to live in Stratford-upon-Avon, where he owned a large house and considerable property, and where his wife and his two daughters lived. (His son Hamnet had died in 1596.) However, other biographers suggest that Shakespeare did not leave London for good until much closer to the time of his death. During his professional years in London, Shakespeare had presumably derived income from the acting company's profits as well as from his own career as an actor, from the sale of his play manuscripts to the acting company, and, after 1599, from his shares as an owner of the Globe. It was presumably that income, carefully invested in land and other property, that made him the wealthy man that surviving documents show him to have become. It is also assumed that William Shakespeare's growing wealth and reputation played some part in inclining the Crown, in 1596, to grant John Shakespeare, William's father, the coat of arms that he had so long sought. William Shake-

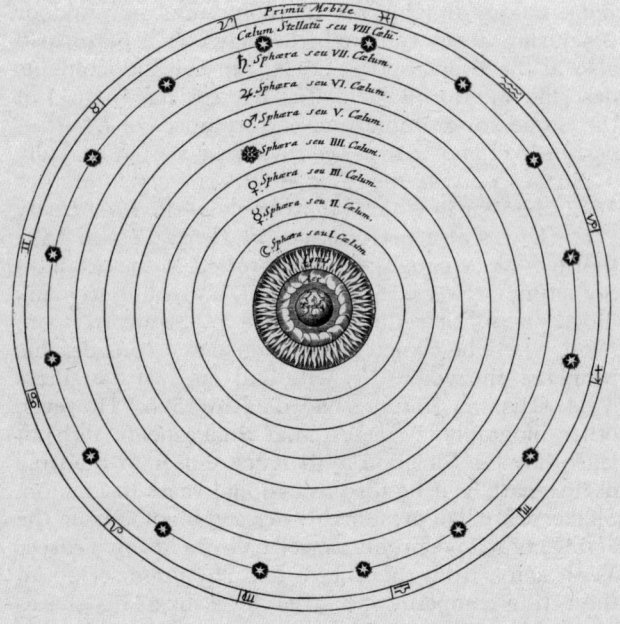

Ptolemaic universe.
From Marcus Manilius, *The sphere of* . . . (1675).

speare died in Stratford on April 23, 1616 (according to the epitaph carved under his bust in Holy Trinity Church) and was buried on April 25. Seven years after his death, his collected plays were published as *Mr. William Shakespeares Comedies, Histories, & Tragedies* (the work now known as the First Folio).

The years in which Shakespeare wrote were among the most exciting in English history. Intellectually, the discovery, translation, and printing of Greek and Roman classics were making available a set of works and worldviews that interacted complexly with Christian texts and beliefs. The result was a questioning, a vital intellectual ferment, that provided energy for the period's amazing dramatic and literary output and that fed directly into Shakespeare's plays. The Ghost in *Hamlet*, for example, is wonderfully complicated in part because he is a figure from Roman tragedy— the spirit of the dead returning to seek revenge—who at the same time inhabits a Christian hell (or purgatory); Hamlet's description of humankind reflects at one moment the Neoplatonic wonderment at mankind ("What a piece of work is a man!") and, at the next, the Christian view of the human condition ("And yet, to me, what is this quintessence of dust?").

As intellectual horizons expanded, so also did geographical and cosmological horizons. New worlds— both North and South America—were explored, and in them were found human beings who lived and worshiped in ways radically different from those of Renaissance Europeans and Englishmen. The universe during these years also seemed to shift and expand. Copernicus had earlier theorized that the earth was not the center of the cosmos but revolved as a planet around the sun. Galileo's telescope, created in 1609, allowed scientists to see that Copernicus had been correct: the universe was not organized with the earth at the center, nor was it so nicely circumscribed as people had, until that time, thought. In terms of expanding horizons, the impact of these discoveries on people's beliefs—religious, scientific, and philosophical—cannot be overstated.

London, too, rapidly expanded and changed during the years (from the early 1590s to around 1610) that Shakespeare lived there. London—the center of England's government, its economy, its royal court, its overseas trade—was, during these years, becoming an exciting metropolis, drawing to it thousands of new citizens every year. Troubled by overcrowding, by poverty, by recurring epidemics of the plague, London was also a mecca for the wealthy and the aristocratic, and for those who sought advancement at court, or power in government or finance or trade. One hears in Shakespeare's plays the voices of London—the struggles for power, the fear of venereal disease, the language of buying and selling. One hears as well the voices of Stratford-upon-Avon—references to the nearby Forest of Arden, to sheepherding, to small-town gossip, to village fairs and markets. Part of the richness of Shakespeare's work is the influence felt there of the various worlds in which he lived: the world of metropolitan London, the world of small-town and rural England, the world of the theater, and the worlds of craftsmen and shepherds.

That Shakespeare inhabited such worlds we know from surviving London and Stratford documents, as well as from the evidence of the plays and poems themselves. From such records we can sketch the dramatist's life. We know from his works that he was a voracious reader. We know from legal and business documents that he was a multifaceted theater man who became a wealthy landowner. We know a bit about his family life and a fair amount about his legal and financial dealings. Most scholars today depend upon such evidence as they draw their picture of the world's greatest playwright. Such, however, has not always been the case. Until the late eighteenth century, the William Shakespeare who lived in most biographies was the creation of legend and tradition. This was the Shakespeare who was supposedly caught poaching deer at Charlecote, the estate of Sir Thomas Lucy close by Stratford; this was the Shakespeare who fled from Sir Thomas's vengeance and made his way in London by taking care of horses outside a playhouse; this was the Shakespeare who reportedly could barely read, but whose natural gifts were extraordinary, whose father was a butcher who allowed his gifted son sometimes to help in the butcher shop, where William supposedly killed calves "in a high style," making a speech for the occasion. It was this legendary William Shakespeare whose Falstaff (in *1* and *2 Henry IV*) so pleased Queen Elizabeth that she demanded a play about Falstaff in love, and demanded that it be written in fourteen days (hence the existence of *The Merry Wives of Windsor*). It was this legendary Shakespeare who reached the top of his acting career in the roles of the Ghost in *Hamlet* and old Adam in *As You Like It*—and who died of a fever contracted by drinking too hard at "a merry meeting" with the poets Michael Drayton and Ben Jonson. This legendary Shakespeare is a rambunctious, undisciplined man, as attractively "wild" as his plays were seen by earlier generations to be. Unfortunately, there is no trace of evidence to support these wonderful stories.

Perhaps in response to the disreputable Shakespeare of legend—or perhaps in response to the fragmentary and, for some, all-too-ordinary Shakespeare documented by surviving records—some people since the mid-nineteenth century have argued that William Shakespeare could not have written the plays that bear his name. These persons have put forward some dozen names as more likely authors, among them Queen Elizabeth, Sir Francis Bacon, Edward de Vere (earl of Oxford), and Christopher Marlowe. Such attempts to find what for these people is a more believable author of the plays is a tribute to the regard in which the plays are held. Unfortunately for their claims, the documents that exist that provide evidence for the facts of Shakespeare's life tie him inextricably to the body of plays and poems that bear his name. Unlikely as it seems to those who want the works to have been written by an aristocrat, a university graduate, or an "important" person, the plays and poems seem clearly to have been produced by a man from Stratford-upon-Avon with a very good "grammar-school" education and a life of experience in London and in the world of the London theater. How this particular man produced the works that dominate the cultures of much of the world almost four hundred years after his death is one of life's mysteries—and one that will continue to tease our imaginations as we continue to delight in his plays and poems.

Shakespeare's Theater

The actors of Shakespeare's time are known to have performed plays in a great variety of locations. They played at court (that is, in the great halls of such royal residences as Whitehall, Hampton Court, and Greenwich); they played in halls at the universities of Oxford and Cambridge, and at the Inns of Court (the residences in London of the legal societies); and they also played in the private houses of great lords and civic officials. Sometimes acting companies went on tour from London into the provinces, often (but not only) when outbreaks of bubonic plague in the capital forced the closing of theaters to reduce the possibility of contagion in crowded audiences. In the provinces the actors usually staged their plays in churches (until around 1600) or in guildhalls. While surviving records show only a handful of occasions when actors played at inns while on tour, London inns were important playing places up until the 1590s.

The building of theaters in London had begun only shortly before Shakespeare wrote his first plays in the 1590s. These theaters were of two kinds: outdoor or public playhouses that could accommodate large numbers of playgoers, and indoor or private theaters for much smaller audiences. What is usually regarded as the first London outdoor public playhouse was called simply the Theatre. James Burbage—the father of Richard Burbage, who was perhaps the most famous actor in Shakespeare's company—built it in 1576 in an area north of the city of London called Shoreditch. Among the more famous of the other public playhouses that capitalized on the new fashion were the Curtain and the Fortune (both also built north of the city), the Rose,

A stylized representation of the Globe theater.
From Claes Jansz Visscher, *Londinum florentissima
Britanniae urbs . . .* [c. 1625].

the Swan, the Globe, and the Hope (all located on the Bankside, a region just across the Thames south of the city of London). All these playhouses had to be built outside the jurisdiction of the city of London because many civic officials were hostile to the performance of drama and repeatedly petitioned the royal council to abolish it.

The theaters erected on the Bankside (a region under the authority of the Church of England, whose head was the monarch) shared the neighborhood with houses of prostitution and with the Paris Garden, where the blood sports of bearbaiting and bullbaiting were carried on. There may have been no clear distinction between playhouses and buildings for such sports, for we know that the Hope was used for both plays and baiting and that Philip Henslowe, owner of the Rose and, later, partner in the ownership of the Fortune, was also a partner in a monopoly on baiting. All these forms of entertainment were easily accessible to Londoners by boat across the Thames or over London Bridge.

Evidently Shakespeare's company prospered on the Bankside. They moved there in 1599. Threatened by difficulties in renewing the lease on the land where their first theater (the Theatre) had been built, Shakespeare's company took advantage of the Christmas holiday in 1598 to dismantle the Theatre and transport its timbers across the Thames to the Bankside, where, in 1599, these timbers were used in the building of the Globe. The weather in late December 1598 is recorded as having been especially harsh. It was so cold that the Thames was "nigh [nearly] frozen," and there was heavy snow. Perhaps the weather aided Shakespeare's company in eluding their landlord, the snow hiding their activity and the freezing of the Thames allowing them to slide the timbers across to the Bankside without paying tolls for repeated trips over London

Bridge. Attractive as this narrative is, it remains just as likely that the heavy snow hampered transport of the timbers in wagons through the London streets to the river. It also must be remembered that the Thames was, according to report, only "nigh frozen," and therefore did not necessarily provide solid footing. Whatever the precise circumstances of this fascinating event in English theater history, Shakespeare's company was able to begin playing at their new Globe theater on the Bankside in 1599. After this theater burned down in 1613 during the staging of Shakespeare's *Henry VIII* (its thatch roof was set alight by cannon fire called for in performance), Shakespeare's company immediately rebuilt on the same location. The second Globe seems to have been a grander structure than its predecessor. It remained in use until the beginning of the English Civil War in 1642, when Parliament officially closed the theaters. Soon thereafter it was pulled down.

The public theaters of Shakespeare's time were very different buildings from our theaters today. First of all, they were open-air playhouses. As recent excavations of the Rose and the Globe confirm, some were polygonal or roughly circular in shape; the Fortune, however, was square. The most recent estimates of their size put the diameter of these buildings at 72 feet (the Rose) to 100 feet (the Globe), but we know that they held vast audiences of two or three thousand, who must have been squeezed together quite tightly. Some of these spectators paid extra to sit or stand in the two or three levels of roofed galleries that extended, on the upper levels, all the way around the theater and surrounded an open space. In this space were the stage and, perhaps, the tiring house (what we would call dressing rooms), as well as the so-called yard. In the yard stood the spectators who chose to pay less, the ones whom Hamlet contemptuously called "groundlings." For a roof they had only the sky, and so they were exposed to all kinds of weather. They stood on a floor that was sometimes made of mortar and sometimes of ash mixed with the shells of hazelnuts, which, it has recently been discovered, were standard flooring material in the period.

Unlike the yard, the stage itself was covered by a roof. Its ceiling, called "the heavens," is thought to have been elaborately painted to depict the sun, moon, stars, and planets. The exact size of the stage remains hard to determine. We have a single sketch of part of the interior of the Swan. A Dutchman named Johannes de Witt visited this theater around 1596 and sent a sketch of it back to his friend, Arend van Buchel. Because van Buchel found de Witt's letter and sketch of interest, he copied both into a book. It is van Buchel's copy, adapted, it seems, to the shape and size of the page in his book, that survives. In this sketch, the stage appears to be a large rectangular platform that thrusts far out into the yard, perhaps even as far as the center of the circle formed by the surrounding galleries. This drawing, combined with the specifications for the size of the stage in the building contract for the Fortune, has led scholars to conjecture that the stage on which Shakespeare's plays were performed must have measured approximately 43 feet in width and 27 feet in depth, a vast acting area. But the digging up of a large part of the Rose by late twentieth-century archaeologists has provided evidence of a quite different stage design. The Rose stage was a platform tapered at the corners and much shallower than what seems to be depicted in the van Buchel sketch. Indeed, its measurements seem to be about 37.5 feet across at its widest point and only 15.5 feet deep. Because the surviving indications of stage size and design differ from each other so much, it is possible that the stages in other theaters, like the Theatre, the Curtain, and the Globe (the outdoor playhouses where we know that Shakespeare's plays were performed), were different from those at both the Swan and the Rose.

After about 1608 Shakespeare's plays were staged not only at the Globe but also at an indoor or private playhouse in Blackfriars. This theater had been constructed in 1596 by James Burbage in an upper hall of a former Dominican priory or monastic house. Although Henry VIII had dissolved all English monasteries in the 1530s (shortly after he had founded the Church of England), the area remained under church, rather than hostile civic, control. The hall that Burbage had purchased and renovated was a large one in which Parliament had once met. In the private theater that he constructed, the stage, lit by candles, was built across the narrow end of the hall, with boxes flanking it. The rest of the hall offered seating room only. Because there was no provision for standing room, the largest audience it could hold was less than a thousand, or about a quarter of what the Globe could accommodate. Admission to Blackfriars was correspondingly more expensive. Instead of a penny to stand in the yard at the Globe, it cost a minimum of sixpence to get into Blackfriars. The best seats at the Globe (in the Lords' Room in the gallery above and behind the stage) cost sixpence; but the boxes flanking the stage at Blackfriars were half a crown, or five times sixpence. Some spectators who were particularly interested in displaying themselves paid even more to sit on stools on the Blackfriars stage.

Whether in the outdoor or indoor playhouses, the stages of Shakespeare's time were different from ours. They were not separated from the audience by the dropping of a curtain between acts and scenes. Therefore the playwrights of the time had to find other ways of signaling to the audience that one scene (to be imagined as occurring in one location at a given time) had ended and the next (to be imagined at perhaps a different location at a later time) had begun. The customary way used by Shakespeare and many of his contemporaries was to have everyone on stage exit at the end of one scene and have one or more different characters enter to begin the next. In a few cases, where characters remain onstage from one scene to another, the dialogue or stage action makes the change of location clear, and the characters are generally to be imagined as having moved from one place to another. For example, in *Romeo and Juliet,* Romeo and his friends remain onstage in Act 1 from scene 4 to scene 5, but they are represented as having moved between scenes from the street that leads to Capulet's house into Capulet's house itself. The new location is signaled in part by the appearance onstage of Capulet's servingmen carrying table napkins, something they would not take into the streets. Playwrights had to be quite resourceful in the use of hand properties, like the napkin, or in the use of dialogue to specify where the action was taking place in their plays because, in contrast to most of today's theaters, the playhouses of Shakespeare's time did not fill the stage with scenery to make the setting precise. A consequence of this difference was that the playwrights of Shakespeare's time did not have to specify exactly where the action of their plays was set when they did not choose to do so, and much of the action of their plays is tied to no specific place.

Usually Shakespeare's stage is referred to as a "bare stage," to distinguish it from the stages of the last two or three centuries with their elaborate sets. But the stage in Shakespeare's time was not completely bare. Philip Henslowe, owner of the Rose, lists in his inventory of stage properties a rock, three tombs, and two mossy banks. Stage directions in plays of the time also call for such things as thrones (or "states"), banquets (presumably tables with plaster replicas of food on them), and beds and tombs to be pushed onto the stage. Thus the stage often held more than the actors.

The actors did not limit their performing to the stage alone. Occasionally they went beneath the stage, as the Ghost appears to do in the first act of *Hamlet*. From there they could emerge onto the stage through a trapdoor. They could retire behind the hangings across the back of the stage, as, for example, the actor playing Polonius does when he hides behind the arras. Sometimes the hangings could be drawn back during a performance to "discover" one or more actors behind them. When performance required that an actor appear "above," as when Juliet is imagined to stand at the window of her chamber in the famous and misnamed "balcony scene," then the actor probably climbed the stairs to the gallery over the back of the stage and temporarily shared it with some of the spectators. The stage was also provided with ropes and winches so that actors could descend from, and reascend to, the "heavens."

Perhaps the greatest difference between dramatic performances in Shakespeare's time and ours was that in Shakespeare's England the roles of women were played by boys. (Some of these boys grew up to take male roles in their maturity.) There were no women in the acting companies. It was not so in Europe, and it had not always been so in the history of the English stage. There are records of women on English stages in the thirteenth and fourteenth centuries, two hundred years before Shakespeare's plays were performed. After the accession of James I in 1603, the queen of England and her ladies took part in entertainments at court called masques, and with the reopening of the theaters in 1660 at the restoration of Charles II, women again took their place on the public stage.

The chief competitors of such acting companies as the one to which Shakespeare belonged and for which he wrote were companies of exclusively boy actors. The competition was most intense in the early 1600s. There were then two principal children's companies: the Children of Paul's (the choirboys from St. Paul's Cathedral, whose private playhouse was near the cathedral); and the Children of the Chapel Royal (the choirboys from the monarch's private chapel, who performed at the Blackfriars theater built by Burbage in 1596). In *Hamlet* Shakespeare writes of "an aerie [nest] of children, little eyases [hawks], that cry out on the top of question and are most tyrannically clapped for 't. These are now the fashion and . . . berattle the common stages [attack the public theaters]." In the long run, the adult actors prevailed. The Children of Paul's dissolved around 1606. By about 1608 the Children of the Chapel Royal had been forced to stop playing at the Blackfriars theater, which was then taken over by the King's Men, Shakespeare's own troupe.

Acting companies and theaters of Shakespeare's time seem to have been organized in various ways. For example, with the building of the Globe, Shakespeare's company apparently managed itself, with the principal actors, Shakespeare among them, having the status of "sharers" and the right to a share in the takings, as well as the responsibility for a part of the expenses. Five of the sharers, including Shakespeare, owned the Globe. As actor, as sharer in an acting company and in ownership of theaters, and as playwright, Shakespeare was about as involved in the theatrical industry as one could imagine. Although Shakespeare and his fellows prospered, their status under the law was conditional upon the protection of powerful patrons. "Common players"—those who did not have patrons or masters—were classed in the language of the law with "vagabonds and sturdy beggars." So the actors had to secure for themselves the official rank of servants of patrons. Among the patrons under whose protection Shakespeare's company worked were the lord chamberlain and, after the accession of King James in 1603, the king himself.

In the early 1990s we began to learn a great deal more about the theaters in which Shakespeare and his contemporaries performed—or, at least, began to open up new questions about them. At that time about 70 percent of the Rose had been excavated, as had about 10 percent of the second Globe, the one built in 1614. Excavation was halted at that point, but London has come to value the sites of its early playhouses, and takes what opportunities it can to explore them more deeply, both on the Bankside and in Shoreditch. Information about the playhouses of Shakespeare's London is therefore a constantly changing resource.

The Publication of Shakespeare's Plays

Eighteen of Shakespeare's plays found their way into print during the playwright's lifetime, but there is nothing to suggest that he took any interest in their publication. These eighteen appeared separately in editions in quarto or, in the case of *Henry VI, Part 3*, octavo format. The quarto pages are not much larger than a modern mass-market paperback book, and the octavo pages are even smaller; these little books were sold unbound for a few pence. The earliest of the quartos that still survive were printed in 1594, the year that both *Titus Andronicus* and a version of the play now called *Henry VI, Part 2* became available. While almost every one of these early quartos displays on its title page the name of the acting company that performed the play, only about half provide the name of the playwright, Shakespeare. The first quarto edition to bear the name Shakespeare on its title page is *Love's Labor's Lost* of 1598. A few of the quartos were popular with the book-buying public of Shakespeare's lifetime; for example, quarto *Richard II* went through five editions between 1597 and 1615. But most of the quartos were far from best sellers; *Love's Labor's Lost* (1598), for instance, was not reprinted in quarto until 1631. After Shakespeare's death, two more of his plays appeared in quarto format: *Othello* in 1622 and *The Two Noble Kinsmen*, coauthored with John Fletcher, in 1634.

In 1623, seven years after Shakespeare's death, *Mr. William Shakespeares Comedies, Histories, & Tragedies* was published. This printing offered readers in a single book thirty-six of the thirty-eight plays now thought to have been written by Shakespeare, including eighteen that had never been printed before. And it offered them in a style that was then reserved for serious literature and scholarship. The plays were arranged in double columns on pages nearly a foot high. This large page size is called "folio," as opposed to the smaller "quarto," and the 1623 volume is usually called the Shakespeare First Folio. It is reputed to have sold for the lordly price of a pound. (One copy at the Folger Shakespeare Library is marked fifteen shillings—that is, three-quarters of a pound.)

In a preface to the First Folio entitled "To the great Variety of Readers," two of Shakespeare's former fellow actors in the King's Men, John Heminge and Henry Condell, wrote that they themselves had collected their dead companion's plays. They suggested that they had seen his own papers: "we have scarce received from him a blot in his papers." The title page of the Folio declared that the plays within it had been printed "according to the True Original Copies." Comparing the Folio to the quartos, Heminge and Condell disparaged the quartos, advising their readers that "before you were abused with divers stolen and surreptitious copies, maimed, and deformed by the frauds and stealths of injurious impostors." Many Shakespeareans of the eighteenth and nineteenth centuries believed Heminge and Condell and regarded the Folio plays as superior to anything in the quartos.

Once we begin to examine the Folio plays in detail, it becomes less easy to take at face value the word of Heminge and Condell about the superiority of the Folio texts. For example, of the first nine plays in the Folio (one-quarter of the entire collection), four were essentially reprinted from earlier quarto printings that Heminge and Condell had disparaged, and four have now been identified as printed from copies written in the hand of a professional scribe of the 1620s named Ralph Crane; the ninth, *The Comedy of Errors*, was apparently also printed from a manuscript, but one whose origin cannot be readily identified. Evidently, then, eight of the first nine plays in the First Folio were not printed, in spite of what the Folio title page announces, "according to the True Original Copies," or Shakespeare's own papers, and the source of the ninth is unknown. Since today's editors have been forced to treat Heminge and Condell's pronouncements with skepticism, they must choose whether to base their own editions upon quartos or the Folio on grounds other than Heminge and Condell's story of where the quarto and Folio versions originated.

Editors have often fashioned their own narratives to explain what lies behind the quartos and Folio. They have said that Heminge and Condell meant to criticize only a few of the early quartos, the ones that offer much shorter and sometimes quite different, often garbled, versions of plays. Among the examples of these are the 1600 quarto of *Henry V* (the Folio offers a much fuller version) or the 1603 *Hamlet* quarto. (In 1604 a different, much longer form of the play got into print as a quarto.) Early twentieth-century editors speculated that these questionable texts were produced when someone in the audience took notes from the plays' dialogue during performances and then employed "hack poets" to fill out the notes. The poor results were then sold to a publisher and presented in print as Shakespeare's plays. More recently this story has given way to another in which the shorter versions are said to be re-creations from memory of Shakespeare's plays by actors who wanted to stage them in the provinces but lacked manuscript copies. Most of the quartos offer much better texts than these so-called bad quartos. Indeed, in most of the quartos we find texts that are at least equal to or better than what is printed in the Folio. Many Shakespeare enthusiasts persuaded themselves that most of the quartos were set into type directly from Shakespeare's own papers, although there is nothing on which to base this conclusion except the desire for it to be true. Thus speculation continues about how the Shakespeare plays got to be printed. All that we have are the printed texts.

The book collector who was most successful in bringing together copies of the quartos and the First Folio was Henry Clay Folger, founder of the Folger Shakespeare Library in Washington, D.C. While it is estimated that there survive around the world only about 230 copies of the First Folio, Mr. Folger was able to acquire more than seventy-five copies, as well as a large number of fragments, for the library that bears his name. He also amassed a substantial number of quartos. For example, only fourteen copies of the First Quarto of *Love's Labor's Lost* are known to exist, and three are at the Folger Shakespeare Library. As a consequence of Mr. Folger's labors, scholars visiting the Folger Shakespeare Library have been able to learn a great deal about sixteenth- and seventeenth-century printing and, particularly, about the printing of Shakespeare's plays. And Mr. Folger did not stop at the First Folio, but collected many copies of later editions of Shakespeare, beginning with the Second Folio (1632), the Third (1663–64), and the Fourth (1685). Each of these later folios was based on its immediate predecessor and was edited anonymously. The first editor of Shakespeare whose name we know was Nicholas Rowe, whose first edition came out in 1709. Mr. Folger collected this edition and many, many more by Rowe's successors, and the collecting and scholarship continue.

An Introduction to This Text

The Tempest was first printed in the 1623 collection of Shakespeare's plays now known as the First Folio. The present edition is based directly upon that printing.* *The Tempest* is the first of the plays in the First Folio, and there is every indication that the printer of the book took special care in its printing so as to attract buyers to the large and expensive book. For printer's copy for the play he seems to have employed a transcript by the scribe Ralph Crane, whose manuscripts of a number of other plays by Shakespeare's contemporaries survive. These are beautiful works of scribal art and are largely free from obvious errors. Use of a Crane transcript would have eased the work of the First Folio typesetters and would have enabled them to produce a very clean text. However, we can identify their printer's copy as Crane's work only because he left his own marks on the plays he copied. From what we know of this work, we must suspect that the punctuation, stage directions, cast of characters, act and scene divisions, and many contractions of words to affect meter are probably Crane's, and that some of the dialogue may contain emendations of words not to Crane's liking. To improve the appearance of *The Tempest* in the First Folio, the printer was also careful to catch and correct errors that made their way into print. For example, the first page of the play has been found in copies of the First Folio in four different states of correction that show that the printer stopped the press three times

---

*We have also consulted the computerized text of the First Folio provided by the Text Archive of the Oxford University Computing Centre, to which we are grateful.

during the print run in order to fix mistakes. As a consequence of using a Crane manuscript as printer's copy and of repeated proof-reading, the First Folio text of *The Tempest* exhibits few readily identifiable errors for editors to correct.

For the convenience of the reader, we have modernized the punctuation and the spelling of the Folio. Sometimes we go so far as to modernize certain old forms of words; for example, when *a* means "he," we change it to *he;* we change *mo* to *more,* and *ye* to *you.* But it is not our practice in editing any of the plays to modernize words that sound distinctly different from modern forms. For example, when the early printed texts read *sith* or *apricocks* or *porpentine,* we have not modernized to *since, apricots, porcupine.* When the forms *an, and,* or *and if* appear instead of the modern form *if,* we have reduced *and* to *an* but have not changed any of these forms to their modern equivalent, *if.* We also modernize and, where necessary, correct passages in foreign languages, unless an error in the early printed text can be reasonably explained as a joke.

Whenever we change the wording of the First Folio or add anything to its stage directions, we mark the change by enclosing it in superior half-brackets (⌐¬). We want our readers to be immediately aware when we have intervened. (Only when we correct an obvious typographical error in the First Folio does the change not get marked.) Whenever we change the First Folio's wording or its punctuation so that meaning changes, we list the change in the textual notes at the back of the book, even if all we have done is fix an obvious error.

We regularize a number of the proper names, as is the usual practice in editions of the play. For example, the Folio once names the Boatswain the "Boson," a form that is interesting for its reproduction of the word's pronunciation; nevertheless, we regularize this spelling to *boatswain*. The Folio often employs the spelling *Anthonio* for *Antonio* in stage directions and speech headings, but this edition is consistent in using only *Antonio*.

This edition differs from many earlier ones in its efforts to aid the reader in imagining the play as a performance. Thus stage directions are written with reference to the stage. For example, many earlier editions add the following stage direction to the play's last scene to describe an important piece of stage business: *"Prospero draws a magic circle with his staff."* Because, in a stage production, the circle drawn by the actor is, of course, not "magic" at all, we instead print the following stage direction: *"Prospero draws a large circle on the stage with his staff."* Whenever it is reasonably certain, in our view, that a speech is accompanied by a particular action, we provide a stage direction describing the action. (Occasional exceptions to this rule occur when the action is so obvious that to add a stage direction would insult the reader.) Stage directions for the entrance of characters in mid-scene are, with rare exceptions, placed so that they immediately precede the characters' participation in the scene, even though these entrances may appear somewhat earlier in the early printed texts. Whenever we move a stage direction, we record this change in the textual notes. Latin stage directions (e.g., *Exeunt*) are translated into English (e.g., *They exit*).

We expand the often severely abbreviated forms of names used as speech headings in early printed texts into the full names of the characters. We also regularize the speakers' names in speech headings, using only a single designation for each character, even though the early printed texts sometimes use a variety of designations. Variations in the speech headings of the early printed texts are recorded in the textual notes.

In the present edition, as well, we mark with a dash any change of address within a speech, unless a stage direction intervenes. When the *-ed* ending of a word is to be pronounced, we mark it with an accent. Like editors for the past two centuries we print metrically linked lines in the following way:

PROSPERO
    But are they, Ariel, safe?
ARIEL   Not a hair perished.
                 (1.2.257–58)

However, when there are a number of short verse lines that can be linked in more than one way, we do not, with rare exceptions, indent any of them.

The Explanatory Notes

The notes that appear on the pages facing the text are designed to provide readers with the help they may need to enjoy the play. Whenever the meaning of a word in the text is not readily accessible in a good contemporary dictionary, we offer the meaning in a note. Sometimes we provide a note even when the relevant meaning is to be found in the dictionary but when the word has acquired since Shakespeare's time other potentially confusing meanings. In our notes, we try to offer modern synonyms for Shakespeare's words. We also try to indicate to the reader the connection between the word in the play and the modern synonym. For example, Shakespeare sometimes uses the word *head* to mean "source," but, for modern readers, there may be no connection evident between these two words. We provide the connection by explaining Shakespeare's usage as follows: "**head:** fountainhead, source." On some occasions, a whole phrase or clause needs explanation. Then we rephrase in our own words the difficult passage, and add at the end synonyms for individual words in the passage. When scholars have been unable to determine the meaning of a word or a phrase, we acknowledge the uncertainty. Unless otherwise noted, biblical quotations are from the Geneva Bible (1560), with spelling and punctuation modernized.

THE TEMPEST

The Scene, an vn-inhabited Island

Names of the Actors.

Alonso, K. of Naples:
Sebastian his Brother.
Prospero, the right Duke of Millaine.
Anthonio his brother, the vsurping Duke of Millaine.
Ferdinand, Son to the King of Naples.
Gonzalo, an honest old Councellor.
Adrian, & Francisco, Lords.
Caliban, a saluage and deformed slaue.
Trinculo, a Iester.
Stephano, a drunken Butler.
Master of a Ship.
Boate-Swaine.
Marriners.
Miranda, daughter to Prospero.
Ariell, an ayrie spirit.

Iris
Ceres
Iuno } *Spirits.*
Nymphes
Reapers

The Tempest cast of characters in the 1623 First Folio
(copy 9, sig. B4ʳ).
From the Folger Shakespeare Library collection.

The Characters in the Play

PROSPERO, the former duke of Milan, now a magician on a Mediterranean island

MIRANDA, Prospero's daughter
ARIEL, a spirit, servant to Prospero
CALIBAN, an inhabitant of the island, servant to Prospero

FERDINAND, prince of Naples

ALONSO, king of Naples
ANTONIO, duke of Milan and Prospero's brother
SEBASTIAN, Alonso's brother
GONZALO, councillor to Alonso and friend to Prospero
ADRIAN
FRANCISCO } courtiers in attendance on Alonso

TRINCULO, servant to Alonso
STEPHANO, Alonso's butler

SHIPMASTER
BOATSWAIN
MARINERS

Players who, as spirits, take the roles of Iris, Ceres, Juno, Nymphs, and Reapers in Prospero's masque, and who, in other scenes, take the roles of "islanders" and of hunting dogs

THE TEMPEST

ACT 1

1.1 On board a ship carrying King Alonso of Naples and his entourage, a boatswain directs the crew to fight a great storm, but the ship appears destined to sink.

---

1. **Boatswain:** pronounced "bòsun."
3. **Good:** i.e., goodman (See also lines 15 and 19.) **yarely:** quickly, nimbly
5. **hearts:** hearties, good fellows
6. **Tend:** pay attention to
7. **Blow:** addressed to the storm; **burst thy wind:** The winds are often pictured as faces puffing out their cheeks (threatening to make them **burst**) as they **blow.** (See picture, page 8.)
7–8. **if room enough:** i.e., so long as we have enough sea room to avoid running aground
10. **Play the men:** If addressed to the boatswain, this would mean "make **the men** do their work"; if addressed to the mariners, it would mean "act like **men.**"
14. **Keep:** i.e., stay in
15. **patient:** calm

ACT 1

Scene 1

A tempestuous noise of thunder and lightning heard.
Enter a Shipmaster and a Boatswain.

MASTER Boatswain!

BOATSWAIN Here, master. What cheer?

MASTER Good, speak to th' mariners. Fall to 't yarely,
or we run ourselves aground. Bestir, bestir!

He exits.

Enter Mariners.

BOATSWAIN Heigh, my hearts! Cheerly, cheerly, my   5
hearts! Yare, yare! Take in the topsail. Tend to th'
Master's whistle.—Blow till thou burst thy wind, if
room enough!

Enter Alonso, Sebastian, Antonio, Ferdinand, Gonzalo,
and others.

ALONSO Good boatswain, have care. Where's the Master? Play the men.   10

BOATSWAIN I pray now, keep below.

ANTONIO Where is the Master, boatswain?

BOATSWAIN Do you not hear him? You mar our labor.
Keep your cabins. You do assist the storm.

GONZALO Nay, good, be patient.   15

BOATSWAIN When the sea is. Hence! What cares these

7

17. **roarers:** i.e., roaring waves (Literally, **roarers** were riotous bullies.)

23. **work . . . present:** perhaps, make **the present** moment peaceful

24. **hand:** handle, lay hold of

29–30. **Methinks:** It seems to me.

30–31. **he hath . . . gallows:** Proverbial: "He who is born to be hanged will not be drowned." **complexion:** appearance (as a reflection of character)

33. **doth little advantage:** i.e., gives us **little** help

36. **Bring her to try:** i.e., make the ship sail close to the wind; **main course:** i.e., mainsail

37 SD. **within:** offstage

37. **A plague upon:** i.e., curses on

38. **office:** i.e., the noise we make in trying to save the ship (literally, duty, assignment)

39. **give o'er:** give up

41. **A pox o':** i.e., curses on

42. **incharitable:** i.e., uncharitable

"Blow till thou burst thy wind." (1.1.7)
From Lodovico Dolce, *Imprese nobili . . .* (1583).

roarers for the name of king? To cabin! Silence! Trouble us not.

GONZALO Good, yet remember whom thou hast aboard. 20

BOATSWAIN None that I more love than myself. You are a councillor; if you can command these elements to silence, and work the peace of the present, we will not hand a rope more. Use your authority. If you cannot, give thanks you have lived so long, and 25 make yourself ready in your cabin for the mischance of the hour, if it so hap.—Cheerly, good hearts!—Out of our way, I say!   *He exits.*

GONZALO I have great comfort from this fellow. Methinks he hath no drowning mark upon him. His 30 complexion is perfect gallows. Stand fast, good Fate, to his hanging. Make the rope of his destiny our cable, for our own doth little advantage. If he be not born to be hanged, our case is miserable.

> *He exits ⌈with Alonso, Sebastian,*
> *and the other courtiers.⌉*

Enter Boatswain.

BOATSWAIN Down with the topmast! Yare! Lower, low- 35 er! Bring her to try wi' th' main course. (*A cry within.*) A plague upon this howling! They are louder than the weather or our office.

Enter Sebastian, Antonio, and Gonzalo.

Yet again? What do you here? Shall we give o'er and drown? Have you a mind to sink? 40

SEBASTIAN A pox o' your throat, you bawling, blasphemous, incharitable dog!

BOATSWAIN Work you, then.

ANTONIO Hang, cur, hang, you whoreson, insolent noisemaker! We are less afraid to be drowned than 45 thou art.

47. **I'll warrant . . . drowning:** i.e., I guarantee he'll not drown (**For** could have the meaning of "against," as it does here.)

49. **unstanched:** unsatisfied, unsated; not made watertight (To *stanch* is to satisfy or to stop the flow of blood or other fluid.)

50. **Lay her ahold:** i.e., bring the ship close to the wind; **Set . . . courses:** i.e., **set** the foresail and mainsail

53. **must our mouths be cold:** i.e., **must** we die (proverbial)

57. **merely:** only; or, completely

58. **wide-chopped:** bigmouthed

61. **glut:** swallow

62 SD. **within:** i.e., offstage

69. **heath:** heather

70. **furze:** shrub (also known as *gorse*); **wills:** i.e., the will of the gods

71. **fain:** rather; gladly

Furze. (1.1.70)
From John Gerard, *The herball . . .* (1597).

GONZALO I'll warrant him for drowning, though the
ship were no stronger than a nutshell and as leaky
as an unstanched wench.
BOATSWAIN Lay her ahold, ahold! Set her two courses.   50
Off to sea again! Lay her off!

Enter ⌜*more*⌝ *Mariners, wet.*

MARINERS All lost! To prayers, to prayers! All lost!
                                        ⌜*Mariners exit.*⌝
BOATSWAIN What, must our mouths be cold?
GONZALO The King and Prince at prayers. Let's assist
them, for our case is as theirs.   55
SEBASTIAN I am out of patience.
ANTONIO We are merely cheated of our lives by drunk-
ards. This wide-chopped rascal—would thou
mightst lie drowning the washing of ten tides!
                                        ⌜*Boatswain exits.*⌝
GONZALO He'll be hanged yet, though every drop of   60
water swear against it and gape at wid'st to glut him.

A confused noise within: "Mercy on us!"—"We split, we
split!"—"Farewell, my wife and children!"—
"Farewell, brother!"—"We split, we split, we
split!"   65

ANTONIO Let's all sink wi' th' King.
SEBASTIAN Let's take leave of him.
                                He exits ⌜*with Antonio.*⌝
GONZALO Now would I give a thousand furlongs of sea
for an acre of barren ground: long heath, brown
furze, anything. The wills above be done, but I   70
would fain die a dry death.
                                                He exits.

1.2 Prospero, the former duke of Milan, who has been stranded on a barren island for twelve years with his daughter, Miranda, explains to her that he used his magic to raise the storm and that he ensured that no one on the ship was harmed. He then tells her how, twelve years before, his brother Antonio conspired with Alonso, king of Naples, to usurp Prospero's dukedom and put him and Miranda to sea, where they happened upon the barren island that is now their home. Having charmed Miranda asleep, Prospero summons the spirit Ariel, hears Ariel's report of the tempest, and gives him further orders. Prospero wakes Miranda, and they visit Caliban, whom Prospero threatens with torture if he will not continue his labors. Ariel, invisible, entices Ferdinand, son and heir to Alonso, into the presence of Prospero and Miranda. Prospero, delighted that Ferdinand and Miranda fall instantly in love, puts false obstacles in their way by accusing Ferdinand of treason and by using charms to enslave him.

———————

1. **art:** learning, skill (specifically, occult learning that gives such magic powers as the ability to control the elements)
4. **welkin's:** sky's
6. **brave:** splendid
7. **Who:** i.e., which
11. **or ere:** before
13. **fraughting souls:** i.e., those who were the ship's freight or cargo
14. **Be collected:** i.e., calm yourself

(continued)

Scene 2
Enter Prospero and Miranda.

MIRANDA
If by your art, my dearest father, you have
Put the wild waters in this roar, allay them.
The sky, it seems, would pour down stinking pitch,
But that the sea, mounting to th' welkin's cheek,
Dashes the fire out. O, I have suffered   5
With those that I saw suffer! A brave vessel,
Who had, no doubt, some noble creature in her,
Dashed all to pieces. O, the cry did knock
Against my very heart! Poor souls, they perished.
Had I been any god of power, I would   10
Have sunk the sea within the earth or ere
It should the good ship so have swallowed, and
The fraughting souls within her.

PROSPERO   Be collected.
No more amazement. Tell your piteous heart   15
There's no harm done.

MIRANDA   O, woe the day!

PROSPERO   No harm.
I have done nothing but in care of thee,
Of thee, my dear one, thee, my daughter, who   20
Art ignorant of what thou art, naught knowing
Of whence I am, nor that I am more better
Than Prospero, master of a full poor cell,
And thy no greater father.

MIRANDA   More to know   25
Did never meddle with my thoughts.

PROSPERO   'Tis time
I should inform thee farther. Lend thy hand
And pluck my magic garment from me.
             ⌈*Putting aside his cloak.*⌉
                  So,   30
Lie there, my art.—Wipe thou thine eyes. Have
   comfort.

15. **amazement:** astonishment, bewilderment; **piteous:** compassionate

19. **but:** except

21. **naught knowing:** i.e., **knowing** nothing

22. **whence I am:** i.e., where I come from; **more better:** i.e., greater

23. **full:** very; **cell:** dwelling consisting of a single chamber inhabited by a hermit or other solitary (The word **cell** could also apply to an animal's cave or to a small cottage or other humble dwelling.)

24. **no greater:** i.e., **no greater** than the **cell** he lives in

31. **art:** magic power (as in 1.2.1)

33. **wrack:** wrecked vessel

34. **virtue:** (1) moral goodness, excellence; (2) power

37. **perdition:** loss

38. **Betid:** happened

39. **Which . . . which:** i.e., whom (i.e., **any creature**) . . . which (i.e., **the vessel**)

44. **bootless:** useless, fruitless

45. **Stay:** wait

51. **Out:** fully

54. **Of anything . . . tell me:** i.e., **tell me the image of anything**

57. **assurance:** objective certainty

58. **remembrance:** memory; **warrants:** guarantees

62. **backward:** past portion (**of time**); **abysm:** abyss

63. **aught:** anything at all; **ere:** before

64. **mayst:** i.e., may remember

The direful spectacle of the wrack, which touched
The very virtue of compassion in thee,
I have with such provision in mine art   35
So safely ordered that there is no soul—
No, not so much perdition as an hair,
Betid to any creature in the vessel
Which thou heard'st cry, which thou saw'st sink. Sit
   down,   40
For thou must now know farther.   ⌜*They sit.*⌝
MIRANDA   You have often
Begun to tell me what I am, but stopped
And left me to a bootless inquisition,
Concluding "Stay. Not yet."   45
PROSPERO   The hour's now come.
The very minute bids thee ope thine ear.
Obey, and be attentive. Canst thou remember
A time before we came unto this cell?
I do not think thou canst, for then thou wast not   50
Out three years old.
MIRANDA   Certainly, sir, I can.
PROSPERO
By what? By any other house or person?
Of anything the image tell me that
Hath kept with thy remembrance.   55
MIRANDA   'Tis far off
And rather like a dream than an assurance
That my remembrance warrants. Had I not
Four or five women once that tended me?
PROSPERO
Thou hadst, and more, Miranda. But how is it   60
That this lives in thy mind? What seest thou else
In the dark backward and abysm of time?
If thou rememb'rest aught ere thou cam'st here,
How thou cam'st here thou mayst.
MIRANDA   But that I do not.   65

66. **Twelve year since:** i.e., **twelve** years ago

67. **Milan:** Throughout the play, this word is pronounced "millen" (with the accent on the first syllable, as in the word "millinery").

68. **prince of power:** i.e., powerful **prince** or ruler

70. **piece:** example (i.e., model)

73. **issued:** i.e., descended

79. **holp:** helped

81. **teen:** trouble; **turned you to:** perhaps, caused you; or, perhaps, made you remember

82. **from:** i.e., away from, not in; **remembrance:** memory

85. **mark:** pay attention to

86. **next:** i.e., next to, second only to

87–88. **to him . . . manage of:** i.e., gave him control of

89. **signories:** lordships, domains; **first:** foremost, best (See note to line 135, below.)

91–92. **for . . . parallel:** i.e., having no equal as a scholar of humanistic studies (The **liberal arts** were the disciplines of grammar, logic, rhetoric, arithmetic, geometry, music, and astronomy.)

94–95. **transported, rapt:** i.e., carried away (as with excitement, emotion, or religious ecstasy)

95. **secret studies:** i.e., study of mystical and occult matters; **false:** treacherous

96. **attend:** pay attention to

PROSPERO
  Twelve year since, Miranda, twelve year since,
  Thy father was the Duke of Milan and
  A prince of power.
MIRANDA   Sir, are not you my father?
PROSPERO
  Thy mother was a piece of virtue, and   70
  She said thou wast my daughter. And thy father
  Was Duke of Milan, and his only heir
  And princess no worse issued.
MIRANDA   O, the heavens!
  What foul play had we that we came from thence?   75
  Or blessèd was 't we did?
PROSPERO   Both, both, my girl.
  By foul play, as thou sayst, were we heaved thence,
  But blessedly holp hither.
MIRANDA   O, my heart bleeds   80
  To think o' th' teen that I have turned you to,
  Which is from my remembrance. Please you,
     farther.
PROSPERO
  My brother and thy uncle, called Antonio—
  I pray thee, mark me—that a brother should   85
  Be so perfidious!—he whom next thyself
  Of all the world I loved, and to him put
  The manage of my state, as at that time
  Through all the signories it was the first,
  And Prospero the prime duke, being so reputed   90
  In dignity, and for the liberal arts
  Without a parallel. Those being all my study,
  The government I cast upon my brother
  And to my state grew stranger, being transported
  And rapt in secret studies. Thy false uncle—   95
  Dost thou attend me?
MIRANDA   Sir, most heedfully.

98. **Being once perfected:** i.e., once he had become a master of; **suits:** petitions, formal requests

100. **trash:** i.e., keep under control (literally, to use a cord or clog in training a hound); **for overtopping:** to prevent the overly ambitious

102–3. **both the key ... office:** i.e., having control over both the governmental positions and the people filling them (**Key** is both "the key to the office" and the musical key to the **tune** that **pleased** Antonio's ear [line 104].)

104. **that:** i.e., so **that**

105. **trunk:** The image here is of Prospero as a tree and Antonio as parasitical **ivy.**

106. **verdure:** flourishing condition, vitality; **out on 't:** i.e., **out**

109. **worldly:** earthly, mundane (i.e., not spiritual)

110. **closeness:** seclusion, solitude

111. **but ... retired:** This phrase means, literally, "except for being so secluded"; here it seems instead to mean "except that it led me into such a secluded life."

112. **O'erprized:** exceeded in value; **popular rate:** the worth accorded it by ordinary people

114. **of:** i.e., in

115. **falsehood:** treachery; **in its contrary:** i.e., (although) in complete opposition (to **my trust**)

117. **sans bound:** i.e., without bounds, limits

119. **But ... exact:** i.e., but also with whatever else **my power might** command

120–21. **Who ... memory:** i.e., **who having made his memory a sinner** against truth by telling **his own lie into:** i.e., unto, against **it:** i.e., his lie

122. **To credit:** i.e., as **to credit** or trust

(continued)

18

PROSPERO
　Being once perfected how to grant suits,
　How to deny them, who t' advance, and who
　To trash for overtopping, new created　　　　　100
　The creatures that were mine, I say, or changed 'em,
　Or else new formed 'em, having both the key
　Of officer and office, set all hearts i' th' state
　To what tune pleased his ear, that now he was
　The ivy which had hid my princely trunk　　　105
　And sucked my verdure out on 't. Thou attend'st not.
MIRANDA
　O, good sir, I do.
PROSPERO　　　　　　I pray thee, mark me.
　I, thus neglecting worldly ends, all dedicated
　To closeness and the bettering of my mind　　110
　With that which, but by being so retired,
　O'erprized all popular rate, in my false brother
　Awaked an evil nature, and my trust,
　Like a good parent, did beget of him
　A falsehood in its contrary as great　　　　　115
　As my trust was, which had indeed no limit,
　A confidence sans bound. He being thus lorded,
　Not only with what my revenue yielded
　But what my power might else exact, like one
　Who, having into truth by telling of it,　　　120
　Made such a sinner of his memory
　To credit his own lie, he did believe
　He was indeed the Duke, out o' th' substitution
　And executing th' outward face of royalty
　With all prerogative. Hence, his ambition growing—　125
　Dost thou hear?
MIRANDA
　Your tale, sir, would cure deafness.
PROSPERO
　To have no screen between this part he played
　And him he played it for, he needs will be

123. **out o’ th’ substitution:** as a result of being my substitute

128. **screen:** i.e., barrier, separation

129. **him . . . for:** i.e., Antonio himself (who wanted to be the duke, not just the duke’s substitute)

130. **Absolute Milan:** i.e., duke of **Milan** with no restrictions or limitations

131. **temporal:** earthly, as opposed to spiritual; **royalties:** privileges and rights belonging to a sovereign

132–33. **confederates . . . wi’:** entered into an agreement with (**Confederates** also carries the sense of “conspires.”)

133. **dry:** thirsty; **sway:** power

135. **his coronet:** i.e., the crown worn by the duke of Milan; **his crown:** i.e., that worn by the king of Naples (Until the nineteenth century, Italy was not a nation but a collection of independent principalities; Milan was a dukedom, Naples a kingdom.)

136. **yet:** until that time; **unbowed:** i.e., independent, unsubjugated (literally, not bowed or bent)

139. **his condition:** i.e., Antonio’s compact (with the king); **th’ event:** i.e., its consequences

141–42. **I . . . grandmother:** i.e., if **I** agree that Antonio is not your brother, **I** would be accusing **my grandmother** of having committed adultery

147. **he:** i.e., the king of Naples; **in lieu o’:** in return for; **premises:** the previously mentioned considerations—a legal term (See lines 134 and 148.)

149. **extirpate:** root up; drive away

155. **ministers:** agents

159. **a hint:** an occasion

163. **now ’s upon ’s:** **now** is **upon** us

164. **impertinent:** irrelevant, not to the point

Absolute Milan. Me, poor man, my library   130
Was dukedom large enough. Of temporal royalties
He thinks me now incapable; confederates,
So dry he was for sway, wi' th' King of Naples
To give him annual tribute, do him homage,
Subject his coronet to his crown, and bend   135
The dukedom, yet unbowed—alas, poor Milan!—
To most ignoble stooping.

MIRANDA   O, the heavens!

PROSPERO
Mark his condition and th' event. Then tell me
If this might be a brother.   140

MIRANDA   I should sin
To think but nobly of my grandmother.
Good wombs have borne bad sons.

PROSPERO   Now the condition.
This King of Naples, being an enemy   145
To me inveterate, hearkens my brother's suit,
Which was that he, in lieu o' th' premises
Of homage and I know not how much tribute,
Should presently extirpate me and mine
Out of the dukedom, and confer fair Milan,   150
With all the honors, on my brother; whereon,
A treacherous army levied, one midnight
Fated to th' purpose did Antonio open
The gates of Milan, and i' th' dead of darkness
The ministers for th' purpose hurried thence   155
Me and thy crying self.

MIRANDA   Alack, for pity!
I, not rememb'ring how I cried out then,
Will cry it o'er again. It is a hint
That wrings mine eyes to 't.   160

PROSPERO   Hear a little further,
And then I'll bring thee to the present business
Which now 's upon 's, without the which this story
Were most impertinent.

165. **Wherefore:** why
167. **demanded:** asked
168. **durst:** dared
169. **nor set:** i.e., **nor** did they dare **set**
171. **ends:** goals
172. **In few:** briefly; **bark:** small sailboat
173. **leagues:** A league is equal to three miles.
174. **a butt:** literally, a cask (for wine or produce)
175. **Nor . . . nor:** i.e., it had neither . . . nor
176. **hoist us:** i.e., put us out to sea (literally, raised us up, as if we were a sail)
182. **cherubin:** cherub, angel (Cherubim were often depicted as rosy-faced, smiling infants with wings. See picture, page 48.)
185. **decked:** adorned; **full salt:** i.e., very salty
186. **which:** i.e., (your) smiles
187. **An undergoing stomach:** a sustaining spirit or temper
193. **charity:** i.e., *caritas,* benevolence
194. **design:** plan; **with:** i.e., along with
195. **stuffs:** woven fabric; or, provisions
196. **steaded much:** i.e., been of great help
197. **gentleness:** nobleness; kindness

MIRANDA   Wherefore did they not   165
  That hour destroy us?
PROSPERO   Well demanded, wench.
  My tale provokes that question. Dear, they durst not,
  So dear the love my people bore me, nor set
  A mark so bloody on the business, but   170
  With colors fairer painted their foul ends.
  In few, they hurried us aboard a bark,
  Bore us some leagues to sea, where they prepared
  A rotten carcass of a butt, not rigged,
  Nor tackle, sail, nor mast; the very rats   175
  Instinctively have quit it. There they hoist us
  To cry to th' sea that roared to us, to sigh
  To th' winds, whose pity, sighing back again,
  Did us but loving wrong.
MIRANDA   Alack, what trouble   180
  Was I then to you!
PROSPERO   O, a cherubin
  Thou wast that did preserve me. Thou didst smile,
  Infusèd with a fortitude from heaven,
  When I have decked the sea with drops full salt,   185
  Under my burden groaned, which raised in me
  An undergoing stomach to bear up
  Against what should ensue.
MIRANDA   How came we ashore?
PROSPERO   By providence divine.   190
  Some food we had, and some fresh water, that
  A noble Neapolitan, Gonzalo,
  Out of his charity, who being then appointed
  Master of this design, did give us, with
  Rich garments, linens, stuffs, and necessaries,   195
  Which since have steaded much. So, of his
    gentleness,
  Knowing I loved my books, he furnished me
  From mine own library with volumes that
  I prize above my dukedom.   200

206. **made . . . profit:** perhaps, **made** you **profit more**; or, perhaps, educated you better

207. **princes:** royal children; **can:** This word perhaps carries its old meaning of "know."

208. **vainer:** more trivial, emptier

214. **Now:** i.e., who is **now**; **my dear lady:** perhaps, my patroness (**Fortune,** who is conventionally pictured as a fickle woman, now looks with kindness on Prospero.)

216. **my zenith:** i.e., my (reaching the) highest point (of good fortune)

217. **influence:** i.e., astrological power

218. **omit:** neglect

220. **dullness:** drowsiness

221. **give it way:** i.e., **give** in to **it**

222. **Come away:** i.e., **come**

224. **Grave:** worthy

227. **task:** (1) put to the task, put to work; (2) put to the test

228. **quality:** (1) abilities; (2) fellows (perhaps even fellow actors)

230. **to point:** completely, to the smallest detail; **bade:** commanded (past tense of "bid")

MIRANDA   Would I might
But ever see that man.
PROSPERO, ⌈*standing*⌉   Now I arise.
Sit still, and hear the last of our sea-sorrow.
Here in this island we arrived, and here   205
Have I, thy schoolmaster, made thee more profit
Than other princes can, that have more time
For vainer hours and tutors not so careful.

MIRANDA
Heavens thank you for 't. And now I pray you, sir—
For still 'tis beating in my mind—your reason   210
For raising this sea storm?
PROSPERO   Know thus far forth:
By accident most strange, bountiful Fortune,
Now my dear lady, hath mine enemies
Brought to this shore; and by my prescience   215
I find my zenith doth depend upon
A most auspicious star, whose influence
If now I court not, but omit, my fortunes
Will ever after droop. Here cease more questions.
Thou art inclined to sleep. 'Tis a good dullness,   220
And give it way. I know thou canst not choose.
                          ⌈*Miranda falls asleep.*
                          Prospero puts on his cloak.⌉
Come away, servant, come. I am ready now.
Approach, my Ariel. Come.

                          Enter Ariel.

ARIEL
All hail, great master! Grave sir, hail! I come
To answer thy best pleasure. Be 't to fly,   225
To swim, to dive into the fire, to ride
On the curled clouds, to thy strong bidding task
Ariel and all his quality.
PROSPERO   Hast thou, spirit,
Performed to point the tempest that I bade thee?   230

232. **beak:** prow

233. **waist:** midship; **deck:** poop **deck** (at the ship's stern)

234. **amazement:** astonishment and terror

234–37. **Sometimes . . . join:** Travel accounts of the period report a mysterious fire ("St. Elmo's fire") that leaped from place to place on sailing ships.

236. **yards:** spars supporting the sails

237. **Jove's lightning:** Jove, king of the gods in Roman mythology, was armed with lightning bolts. (See picture, page 32.)

240. **Neptune:** god of the sea

242. **trident:** three-pronged scepter carried by Neptune (See picture, page 34.)

243. **brave:** fine

244. **firm:** steadfast, steady; **coil:** disturbance

248. **tricks:** foolish acts

249. **quit:** left abruptly

251. **up-staring:** standing on end

259. **sustaining garments:** perhaps, the clothes that buoyed them up on the water

260. **bad'st:** commanded

261. **troops:** groups

264. **odd angle:** solitary out-of-the-way spot

ARIEL   To every article.
  I boarded the King's ship; now on the beak,
  Now in the waist, the deck, in every cabin,
  I flamed amazement. Sometimes I'd divide
  And burn in many places. On the topmast,   235
  The yards, and bowsprit would I flame distinctly,
  Then meet and join. Jove's lightning, the precursors
  O' th' dreadful thunderclaps, more momentary
  And sight-outrunning were not. The fire and cracks
  Of sulfurous roaring the most mighty Neptune   240
  Seem to besiege and make his bold waves tremble,
  Yea, his dread trident shake.
PROSPERO   My brave spirit!
  Who was so firm, so constant, that this coil
  Would not infect his reason?   245
ARIEL   Not a soul
  But felt a fever of the mad, and played
  Some tricks of desperation. All but mariners
  Plunged in the foaming brine and quit the vessel,
  Then all afire with me. The King's son, Ferdinand,   250
  With hair up-staring—then like reeds, not hair—
  Was the first man that leaped; cried "Hell is empty,
  And all the devils are here."
PROSPERO   Why, that's my spirit!
  But was not this nigh shore?   255
ARIEL   Close by, my master.
PROSPERO
  But are they, Ariel, safe?
ARIEL   Not a hair perished.
  On their sustaining garments not a blemish,
  But fresher than before; and, as thou bad'st me,   260
  In troops I have dispersed them 'bout the isle.
  The King's son have I landed by himself,
  Whom I left cooling of the air with sighs
  In an odd angle of the isle, and sitting,
  His arms in this sad knot.   ⌜*He folds his arms.*⌝ 265

272. **still-vexed:** constantly disturbed (with storms); **Bermoothes:** Bermudas

273. **under hatches:** below deck

274. **Who:** whom; **with a charm:** under a sleep-inducing magic spell; **joined . . . labor:** i.e., which combined with the weariness from the hard work they have undergone

275. **for:** i.e., as **for**

277. **float:** sea

279. **wracked:** shipwrecked

281. **charge:** duty

284. **the mid season:** noon

285. **glasses:** i.e., hours (literally, hourglasses)

288. **remember:** remind

289. **performed me:** i.e., **performed**

293. **the time be out:** i.e., your **time** has been served **out** (See longer note, page 173.)

297. **or . . . or:** either . . . or

298. **bate me:** i.e., subtract

An hourglass. (1.2.285)
From August Casimir Redel,
Apophtegmata symbolica . . . (n.d.).

PROSPERO   Of the King's ship,
  The mariners say how thou hast disposed,
  And all the rest o' th' fleet.
ARIEL   Safely in harbor
  Is the King's ship. In the deep nook, where once   270
  Thou called'st me up at midnight to fetch dew
  From the still-vexed Bermoothes, there she's hid;
  The mariners all under hatches stowed,
  Who, with a charm joined to their suffered labor,
  I have left asleep. And for the rest o' th' fleet,   275
  Which I dispersed, they all have met again
  And are upon the Mediterranean float,
  Bound sadly home for Naples,
  Supposing that they saw the King's ship wracked
  And his great person perish.   280
PROSPERO   Ariel, thy charge
  Exactly is performed. But there's more work.
  What is the time o' th' day?
ARIEL   Past the mid season.
PROSPERO
  At least two glasses. The time 'twixt six and now   285
  Must by us both be spent most preciously.
ARIEL
  Is there more toil? Since thou dost give me pains,
  Let me remember thee what thou hast promised,
  Which is not yet performed me.
PROSPERO   How now? Moody?   290
  What is 't thou canst demand?
ARIEL   My liberty.
PROSPERO
  Before the time be out? No more.
ARIEL   I prithee,
  Remember I have done thee worthy service,   295
  Told thee no lies, made no mistakings, served
  Without or grudge or grumblings. Thou did promise
  To bate me a full year.

303. **salt deep:** ocean

309. **envy:** malice

313. **Argier:** Algiers

315. **Once in a month:** i.e., **once a month**

319. **one thing she did:** We are not told what this **one thing** was, but it may have been the fact that she was **with child** (i.e., pregnant [line 322]).

322. **blue-eyed:** In addition to describing eye color, this term described eyes discolored and sunken from exhaustion, weeping, age, or injury.

325. **for thou wast:** i.e., because you were

327. **hests:** behests, commands

328. **ministers:** agents, servants

329. **unmitigable:** unappeasable

Sycorax, "with age . . . grown into a hoop."
(1.2.309–10)
From *Hortus sanitatis . . .* (1536).

PROSPERO   Dost thou forget
  From what a torment I did free thee?   300
ARIEL   No.
PROSPERO
  Thou dost, and think'st it much to tread the ooze
  Of the salt deep,
  To run upon the sharp wind of the North,
  To do me business in the veins o' th' Earth   305
  When it is baked with frost.
ARIEL   I do not, sir.
PROSPERO
  Thou liest, malignant thing. Hast thou forgot
  The foul witch Sycorax, who with age and envy
  Was grown into a hoop? Hast thou forgot her?   310
ARIEL   No, sir.
PROSPERO
  Thou hast. Where was she born? Speak. Tell me.
ARIEL
  Sir, in Argier.
PROSPERO   O, was she so? I must
  Once in a month recount what thou has been,   315
  Which thou forget'st. This damned witch Sycorax,
  For mischiefs manifold, and sorceries terrible
  To enter human hearing, from Argier,
  Thou know'st, was banished. For one thing she did
  They would not take her life. Is not this true?   320
ARIEL   Ay, sir.
PROSPERO
  This blue-eyed hag was hither brought with child
  And here was left by th' sailors. Thou, my slave,
  As thou report'st thyself, was then her servant,
  And for thou wast a spirit too delicate   325
  To act her earthy and abhorred commands,
  Refusing her grand hests, she did confine thee,
  By help of her more potent ministers
  And in her most unmitigable rage,

332. **space:** i.e., **space** of time

333. **vent:** give forth, discharge

334. **As fast . . . strike:** i.e., **as fast as** the blades of the **mill** wheel **strike** the water

335. **Save:** except

342–43. **penetrate . . . bears:** i.e., make even **bears** feel pity

345. **mine art:** i.e., my magic power

349. **more murmur'st:** i.e., complain any more

350. **his:** i.e., its

353. **correspondent:** responsive, obedient

354. **do my spriting gently:** i.e., carry out my spirit-duties without complaining

359. **make . . . sea:** i.e., disguise yourself as a sea **nymph**

"Jove's lightning." (1.2.237; 5.1.54–55)
From Vincenzo Cartari, *Le vere e noue Imagini . . .* (1615).

Into a cloven pine, within which rift 330
Imprisoned thou didst painfully remain
A dozen years; within which space she died
And left thee there, where thou didst vent thy groans
As fast as mill wheels strike. Then was this island
(Save for the son that ⌐she⌐ did litter here, 335
A freckled whelp, hag-born) not honored with
A human shape.

ARIEL   Yes, Caliban, her son.

PROSPERO
Dull thing, I say so; he, that Caliban
Whom now I keep in service. Thou best know'st 340
What torment I did find thee in. Thy groans
Did make wolves howl, and penetrate the breasts
Of ever-angry bears. It was a torment
To lay upon the damned, which Sycorax
Could not again undo. It was mine art, 345
When I arrived and heard thee, that made gape
The pine and let thee out.

ARIEL   I thank thee, master.

PROSPERO
If thou more murmur'st, I will rend an oak
And peg thee in his knotty entrails till 350
Thou hast howled away twelve winters.

ARIEL   Pardon, master.
I will be correspondent to command
And do my spriting gently.

PROSPERO   Do so, and after two days 355
I will discharge thee.

ARIEL   That's my noble master.
What shall I do? Say, what? What shall I do?

PROSPERO
Go make thyself like a nymph o' th' sea. Be subject
To no sight but thine and mine, invisible 360
To every eyeball else. Go, take this shape,

366. **Heaviness:** sleepiness

370. **villain:** This word could describe a lowborn country person; a scoundrel; a servant; or someone evil and depraved. Miranda could be using the word in any or all of these senses.

372. **as 'tis:** i.e., as things are

373. **miss:** do without

374. **offices:** duties

377 SD. **within:** i.e., offstage

380. **quaint:** clever, ingenious

383. **got:** begotten

384. **dam:** mother (a term usually reserved for animals)

387. **southwest:** i.e., southwest wind

Neptune with his trident. (1.2.240–42)
From Johann Basilius Herold, *Heydenweldt* . . . (1554).

And hither come in 't. Go, hence with diligence!
⌐*Ariel*⌐ *exits.*
Awake, dear heart, awake. Thou hast slept well.
Awake. ⌐*Miranda wakes.*⌐

MIRANDA   The strangeness of your story put   365
Heaviness in me.

PROSPERO   Shake it off. Come on,
We'll visit Caliban, my slave, who never
Yields us kind answer.

MIRANDA, ⌐*rising*⌐   'Tis a villain, sir,   370
I do not love to look on.

PROSPERO   But, as 'tis,
We cannot miss him. He does make our fire,
Fetch in our wood, and serves in offices
That profit us.—What ho, slave, Caliban!   375
Thou earth, thou, speak!

CALIBAN, *within*   There's wood enough within.

PROSPERO
Come forth, I say. There's other business for thee.
Come, thou tortoise. When?

Enter Ariel like a water nymph.

Fine apparition! My quaint Ariel,   380
Hark in thine ear.   ⌐*He whispers to Ariel.*⌐

ARIEL   My lord, it shall be done.   *He exits.*

PROSPERO, ⌐*to Caliban*⌐
Thou poisonous slave, got by the devil himself
Upon thy wicked dam, come forth!

Enter Caliban.

CALIBAN
As wicked dew as e'er my mother brushed   385
With raven's feather from unwholesome fen
Drop on you both. A southwest blow on you
And blister you all o'er.

390. **Urchins:** hedgehogs; or, goblins (perhaps in the form of hedgehogs) See picture, page 38.

391. **forth:** i.e., come forth; **at vast:** i.e., in the immense space

392. **pinched:** tormented (See longer note, page 173.)

393. **As thick as honeycomb:** perhaps, covered with pinches **as a honeycomb** is covered with cells

394. **'em:** i.e., them (the cells of the honeycomb)

401. **the bigger light ... the less:** See Genesis 1.16: "God then made two great lights, the greater light to rule the day, and the less light to rule the night."

403. **qualities:** special features

406. **charms:** magic spells

409. **sty me:** pen me up (A sty was a place where pigs were kept.)

410. **In this hard rock:** perhaps, in this cave (See longer note, page 173.)

412. **slave:** rascal, rogue (In other instances, Prospero's use of this word more likely refers to Caliban's status as an enslaved creature.)

413. **stripes:** blows with a whip; **move:** affect

419. **Would 't:** i.e., I wish it

420. **had peopled else:** would otherwise have populated

PROSPERO
  For this, be sure, tonight thou shalt have cramps,
  Side-stitches that shall pen thy breath up. Urchins   390
  Shall ⌐forth at¬ vast of night that they may work
  All exercise on thee. Thou shalt be pinched
  As thick as honeycomb, each pinch more stinging
  Than bees that made 'em.
CALIBAN   I must eat my dinner.   395
  This island's mine by Sycorax, my mother,
  Which thou tak'st from me. When thou cam'st first,
  Thou strok'st me and made much of me, wouldst
    give me
  Water with berries in 't, and teach me how   400
  To name the bigger light and how the less,
  That burn by day and night. And then I loved thee,
  And showed thee all the qualities o' th' isle,
  The fresh springs, brine pits, barren place and
    fertile.   405
  Cursed be I that did so! All the charms
  Of Sycorax, toads, beetles, bats, light on you,
  For I am all the subjects that you have,
  Which first was mine own king; and here you sty me
  In this hard rock, whiles you do keep from me   410
  The rest o' th' island.
PROSPERO   Thou most lying slave,
  Whom stripes may move, not kindness, I have used
    thee,
  Filth as thou art, with humane care, and lodged   415
    thee
  In mine own cell, till thou didst seek to violate
  The honor of my child.
CALIBAN
  O ho, O ho! Would 't had been done!
  Thou didst prevent me. I had peopled else   420
  This isle with Calibans.

423. **Which . . . take:** i.e., who can receive no impression or imprint of virtue

424. **capable of:** able to receive or be affected by; **ill:** evil

431. **race:** inherited disposition

436. **more than:** i.e., something worse than

437. **my . . . on 't:** i.e., the benefit I derive from it

438. **red plague:** perhaps, the bubonic **plague; rid you:** destroy you

439. **learning:** teaching

442. **answer other business:** perform other duties

444. **rack:** i.e., torture as if on a rack (an instrument for tearing the body apart)

446. **That:** i.e., so **that**

451 SD. **invisible:** i.e., not seen by the characters onstage (There existed a stage costume "for to go invisible." However, since Ariel had been told [at lines 360–61] to be "invisible to every eyeball" except Prospero's, the audience may simply have assumed Ariel's invisibility.)

An urchin, or hedgehog. (1.2.390)
From Edward Topsell, *The historie of foure-footed beastes . . .* (1607).

MIRANDA   Abhorrèd slave,
　Which any print of goodness wilt not take,
　Being capable of all ill! I pitied thee,
　Took pains to make thee speak, taught thee each   425
　　hour
　One thing or other. When thou didst not, savage,
　Know thine own meaning, but wouldst gabble like
　A thing most brutish, I endowed thy purposes
　With words that made them known. But thy vile   430
　　race,
　Though thou didst learn, had that in 't which good
　　natures
　Could not abide to be with. Therefore wast thou
　Deservedly confined into this rock,   435
　Who hadst deserved more than a prison.
CALIBAN
　You taught me language, and my profit on 't
　Is I know how to curse. The red plague rid you
　For learning me your language!
PROSPERO   Hagseed, hence!   440
　Fetch us in fuel; and be quick, thou 'rt best,
　To answer other business. Shrugg'st thou, malice?
　If thou neglect'st or dost unwillingly
　What I command, I'll rack thee with old cramps,
　Fill all thy bones with aches, make thee roar   445
　That beasts shall tremble at thy din.
CALIBAN   No, pray thee.
　⌜*Aside.*⌝ I must obey. His art is of such power
　It would control my dam's god, Setebos,
　And make a vassal of him.   450
PROSPERO   So, slave, hence.
                              Caliban exits.

        Enter Ferdinand; and Ariel, invisible,
            playing and singing.

454–55. **kissed . . . whist:** i.e., **kissed the waves** into silence

456. **featly:** nimbly

458. **burden:** refrain, a set of words recurring at the end of each verse

459. **dispersedly:** i.e., not in unison (perhaps, from various places; or, perhaps, discordantly or unharmoniously); **within:** offstage

463. **strain:** tune, melody; **chanticleer:** i.e., rooster (the name of the rooster-hero of Chaucer's "Nun's Priest's Tale")

466. **sure:** i.e., surely; **waits upon:** attends, serves

470. **their fury:** i.e., the **fury** of the waters; **passion:** suffering, strong emotion

471. **air:** melody; **Thence:** i.e., from the **bank** [line 467] beside the water

474. **Full fathom five:** i.e., fully five fathoms (The depth of the sea was measured in fathoms; five fathoms would be 30 feet.)

477. **fade:** decay

480. **knell:** bell tolled for the dead

Song.

ARIEL

> *Come unto these yellow sands,*
> *And then take hands.*
> *Curtsied when you have, and kissed*
> *The wild waves whist.*   455
> *Foot it featly here and there,*
> *And sweet sprites bear*
> *The burden. Hark, hark!*
>   Burden dispersedly, ⌜within:⌝ *Bow-wow.*
> *The watchdogs bark.*   460
>   ⌜*Burden dispersedly, within:*⌝ *Bow-wow.*
> *Hark, hark! I hear*
> *The strain of strutting chanticleer*
> *Cry cock-a-diddle-dow.*

FERDINAND

Where should this music be? I' th' air, or th' earth? 465
It sounds no more; and sure it waits upon
Some god o' th' island. Sitting on a bank,
Weeping again the King my father's wrack,
This music crept by me upon the waters,
Allaying both their fury and my passion   470
With its sweet air. Thence I have followed it,
Or it hath drawn me rather. But 'tis gone.
No, it begins again.

Song.

ARIEL

> *Full fathom five thy father lies.*
> *Of his bones are coral made.*   475
> *Those are pearls that were his eyes.*
> *Nothing of him that doth fade*
> *But doth suffer a sea change*
> *Into something rich and strange.*
> *Sea nymphs hourly ring his knell.*   480
>   Burden, ⌜within:⌝ *Ding dong.*
> *Hark, now I hear them: ding dong bell.*

483. **ditty:** song; **remember:** commemorate

484. **mortal:** human

485. **owes:** owns

486. **The fringèd . . . advance:** i.e., lift your eyelids

490. **carries:** bears; or, displays; **brave:** splendid

492. **such:** i.e., just **such; gallant:** fine gentleman

493. **something:** somewhat

494. **canker:** literally, a worm that destroys rosebuds, plants, etc.

496. **goodly:** handsome

499. **thing divine:** i.e., not just **a goodly person,** as Prospero had suggested

501. **It:** i.e., Prospero's plan for Miranda and Ferdinand

505–9. **Most sure . . . bear me here:** These lines echo those in the *Aeneid* when Aeneas, shipwrecked in Carthage, meets Venus disguised as a girl. (See longer note, pages 173–74.)

506. **Vouchsafe:** i.e., condescend to answer

507. **May know:** i.e., that **I may know**

509. **bear me:** i.e., **bear** myself, conduct myself

511. **maid:** i.e., a human woman and unmarried

FERDINAND
　The ditty does remember my drowned father.
　This is no mortal business, nor no sound
　That the Earth owes. I hear it now above me.　　　485
PROSPERO, ⌜*to Miranda*⌝
　The fringèd curtains of thine eye advance
　And say what thou seest yond.
MIRANDA　　　　　　　　　　　What is 't? A spirit?
　Lord, how it looks about! Believe me, sir,
　It carries a brave form. But 'tis a spirit.　　　490
PROSPERO
　No, wench, it eats and sleeps and hath such senses
　As we have, such. This gallant which thou seest
　Was in the wrack; and, but he's something stained
　With grief—that's beauty's canker—thou might'st
　　call him
　A goodly person. He hath lost his fellows　　　495
　And strays about to find 'em.
MIRANDA　　　　　　　　　I might call him
　A thing divine, for nothing natural
　I ever saw so noble.　　　　　　　　　500
PROSPERO, ⌜*aside*⌝　　　It goes on, I see,
　As my soul prompts it. ⌜*To Ariel.*⌝ Spirit, fine spirit,
　　I'll free thee
　Within two days for this.
FERDINAND, ⌜*seeing Miranda*⌝　Most sure, the goddess　505
　On whom these airs attend!—Vouchsafe my prayer
　May know if you remain upon this island,
　And that you will some good instruction give
　How I may bear me here. My prime request,
　Which I do last pronounce, is—O you wonder!—　510
　If you be maid or no.
MIRANDA　　　　　　　No wonder, sir,
　But certainly a maid.
FERDINAND　　　　　My language! Heavens!

515. **the best . . . speech:** i.e., king of Naples

519. **single:** solitary; sole; weak

520. **He:** i.e., the king of Naples

521. **that he does I weep:** i.e., it is because **he does that I weep; Naples:** i.e., the king of **Naples**

522. **at ebb:** i.e., dry (The image is from the ebb tide, when the water begins to recede.)

526. **his brave son:** This is the only mention of the duke of Milan's (i.e., Antonio's) son. One assumes that Shakespeare decided against developing this character.

530. **changed eyes:** i.e., exchanged **eyes** (i.e., fallen in love)

536. **Pity move:** i.e., may compassion (for me) persuade

541. **Soft:** i.e., wait a minute

542. **either's:** i.e., each other's

544. **uneasy:** difficult; **light:** easy

545. **light:** (seem) trivial, worthless

546. **charge thee:** i.e., order you

547. **attend:** pay attention to; **usurp:** take unlawful possession of

I am the best of them that speak this speech, 515
Were I but where 'tis spoken.
PROSPERO   How? The best?
What wert thou if the King of Naples heard thee?
FERDINAND
A single thing, as I am now, that wonders
To hear thee speak of Naples. He does hear me, 520
And that he does I weep. Myself am Naples,
Who with mine eyes, never since at ebb, beheld
The King my father wracked.
MIRANDA   Alack, for mercy!
FERDINAND
Yes, faith, and all his lords, the Duke of Milan 525
And his brave son being twain.
PROSPERO, ⌜*aside*⌝   The Duke of Milan
And his more braver daughter could control thee,
If now 'twere fit to do 't. At the first sight
They have changed eyes.—Delicate Ariel, 530
I'll set thee free for this. ⌜*To Ferdinand.*⌝ A word,
    good sir.
I fear you have done yourself some wrong. A word.
MIRANDA
Why speaks my father so ungently? This
Is the third man that e'er I saw, the first 535
That e'er I sighed for. Pity move my father
To be inclined my way.
FERDINAND   O, if a virgin,
And your affection not gone forth, I'll make you
The Queen of Naples. 540
PROSPERO   Soft, sir, one word more.
⌜*Aside.*⌝ They are both in either's powers. But this
    swift business
I must uneasy make, lest too light winning
Make the prize light. ⌜*To Ferdinand.*⌝ One word 545
    more. I charge thee
That thou attend me. Thou dost here usurp

548. **The name . . . not:** i.e., **the name** of king, which does not belong to you   **ow'st:** own

552. **ill:** evil; **temple:** i.e., Ferdinand's body (See longer note, page 174).

553. **ill spirit:** i.e., the devil

556. **traitor:** Prospero has charged Ferdinand with trying to overthrow him as lord of the island (lines 548–50).

560. **fresh-brook mussels:** Only sea **mussels** are edible.

563. **entertainment:** service, employment; treatment; also, perhaps, food and drink

564 SD. **charmed from moving:** i.e., put under a magic spell that immobilizes him

567. **gentle:** honorable; **fearful:** threatening, fear-inspiring

568. **What:** an interjection introducing a question or exclamation

569. **foot:** In the hierarchical world of the period, the child is to the father as the **foot** is to the head. Proverbial: "Do not make the **foot** the head."

572. **ward:** defensive position (Ferdinand has been paralyzed with his sword drawn.)

The name thou ow'st not, and hast put thyself
Upon this island as a spy, to win it
From me, the lord on 't.   550
FERDINAND   No, as I am a man!
MIRANDA
There's nothing ill can dwell in such a temple.
If the ill spirit have so fair a house,
Good things will strive to dwell with 't.
PROSPERO, ⌜*to Ferdinand*⌝   Follow me.   555
  ⌜*To Miranda.*⌝ Speak not you for him. He's a traitor.
    ⌜*To Ferdinand.*⌝ Come,
I'll manacle thy neck and feet together.
Sea water shalt thou drink. Thy food shall be
The fresh-brook mussels, withered roots, and husks   560
Wherein the acorn cradled. Follow.
FERDINAND   No,
I will resist such entertainment till
Mine enemy has more power.
           He draws, and is charmed from moving.
MIRANDA   O dear father,   565
Make not too rash a trial of him, for
He's gentle and not fearful.
PROSPERO   What, I say,
My foot my tutor?—Put thy sword up, traitor,
Who mak'st a show, but dar'st not strike, thy   570
  conscience
Is so possessed with guilt. Come from thy ward,
For I can here disarm thee with this stick
And make thy weapon drop.
MIRANDA   Beseech you, father—   575
PROSPERO
Hence! Hang not on my garments.
MIRANDA   Sir, have pity.
I'll be his surety.
PROSPERO   Silence! One word more
Shall make me chide thee, if not hate thee. What,   580

582. **shapes:** creatures; persons (having his appearance)

584. **To:** i.e., compared to

588. **goodlier:** more handsome

590. **nerves:** sinews

596. **light:** easy, not burdensome

598. **All . . . Earth:** i.e., **all** other places on **Earth**

603. **me:** i.e., for me

607. **unwonted:** not customary

609–10. **free . . . winds:** Proverbial: "**Free as** the air."

Cherubim. (1.2.182)
From Martin Luther, *Der zwey und zwentzigste Psalm . . .* (1525).

An advocate for an impostor? Hush.
Thou think'st there is no more such shapes as he,
Having seen but him and Caliban. Foolish wench,
To th' most of men this is a Caliban,
And they to him are angels.   585
MIRANDA   My affections
  Are then most humble. I have no ambition
  To see a goodlier man.
PROSPERO, ⌜to Ferdinand⌝ Come on, obey.
  Thy nerves are in their infancy again   590
  And have no vigor in them.
FERDINAND   So they are.
  My spirits, as in a dream, are all bound up.
  My father's loss, the weakness which I feel,
  The wrack of all my friends, nor this man's threats   595
  To whom I am subdued, are but light to me,
  Might I but through my prison once a day
  Behold this maid. All corners else o' th' Earth
  Let liberty make use of. Space enough
  Have I in such a prison.   600
PROSPERO, ⌜aside⌝   It works.—Come on.—
  Thou hast done well, fine Ariel.—Follow me.
  ⌜To Ariel.⌝ Hark what thou else shalt do me.
MIRANDA, ⌜to Ferdinand⌝   Be of
    comfort.   605
  My father's of a better nature, sir,
  Than he appears by speech. This is unwonted
  Which now came from him.
PROSPERO, ⌜to Ariel⌝   Thou shalt be as free
  As mountain winds; but then exactly do   610
  All points of my command.
ARIEL   To th' syllable.
PROSPERO, ⌜to Ferdinand⌝
  Come follow. ⌜To Miranda.⌝ Speak not for him.
                                              They exit.

THE TEMPEST

ACT 2

2.1 King Alonso and his entourage wander the island in search of Ferdinand. Gonzalo tries unsuccessfully to encourage hope in Alonso of Ferdinand's survival. Then Ariel, invisible, charms asleep all but Antonio and Sebastian. Antonio seizes the occasion to persuade Sebastian to kill King Alonso and Gonzalo and take the throne of Naples. Ariel, invisible, returns to awake Gonzalo, who wakes the rest. They resume their search.

----

3. **beyond:** i.e., more than; **hint:** occasion

5. **masters of some merchant:** probably, the officers of some merchant ship; **the merchant:** the person who owns the goods on the ship

10. **peace:** i.e., please be quiet

12. **porridge:** i.e., pease-porridge, **porridge** made from peas (Antonio puns on Alonso's word **peace,** line 10.)

13. **visitor:** someone from a parish whose duty it is to comfort the sick or suffering, a function Gonzalo is performing; **give him o'er:** abandon him

14. **he's, his:** refer to Gonzalo

17. **One. Tell.:** i.e., it has now struck **one;** count (the rest)

18. **entertained:** attended to, received

19. **th' entertainer:** i.e., the one who accepts (the grief)

20. **A dollar:** Sebastian responds as if, by **entertainer,** Gonzalo had meant "one who amuses others and gets paid for it."

21. **Dolor:** sorrow

ACT 2

Scene 1
Enter Alonso, Sebastian, Antonio, Gonzalo, Adrian,
Francisco, and others.

GONZALO, ⌜*to Alonso*⌝
Beseech you, sir, be merry. You have cause—
So have we all—of joy, for our escape
Is much beyond our loss. Our hint of woe
Is common; every day some sailor's wife,
The masters of some merchant, and the merchant   5
Have just our theme of woe. But for the miracle—
I mean our preservation—few in millions
Can speak like us. Then wisely, good sir, weigh
Our sorrow with our comfort.
ALONSO   Prithee, peace.   10
SEBASTIAN, ⌜*aside to Antonio*⌝   He receives comfort like
cold porridge.
ANTONIO   The visitor will not give him o'er so.
SEBASTIAN   Look, he's winding up the watch of his wit.
By and by it will strike.   15
GONZALO, ⌜*to Alonso*⌝ Sir—
SEBASTIAN   One. Tell.
GONZALO   When every grief is entertained that's of-
fered, comes to th' entertainer—
SEBASTIAN   A dollar.   20
GONZALO   Dolor comes to him indeed. You have spo-
ken truer than you purposed.

27. **spare:** refrain, stop

30. **Which, of he . . . :** perhaps, **which of** the two, **he . . . ;** or, perhaps, **which, he . . .**

35. **A laughter:** i.e., a laugh (Proverb: "He laughs that wins.")

37. **desert:** deserted, uninhabited

44–45. **subtle . . . temperance:** i.e., mild climate

46. **Temperance:** one of the four cardinal virtues, used as a woman's name

55. **lusty:** i.e., flourishing

58. **eye:** tinge, shade

TEMPERANZA.

Temperance. (2.1.46)
From Cesare Ripa, *Noua iconologia . . .* (1618).

SEBASTIAN You have taken it wiselier than I meant you should.

GONZALO, ⌐to Alonso⌐ Therefore, my lord— 25

ANTONIO Fie, what a spendthrift is he of his tongue.

ALONSO, ⌐to Gonzalo⌐ I prithee, spare.

GONZALO Well, I have done. But yet—

SEBASTIAN, ⌐aside to Antonio⌐ He will be talking.

ANTONIO, ⌐aside to Sebastian⌐ Which, of he or Adrian, 30
for a good wager, first begins to crow?

SEBASTIAN The old cock.

ANTONIO The cockerel.

SEBASTIAN Done. The wager?

ANTONIO A laughter. 35

SEBASTIAN A match!

ADRIAN Though this island seem to be desert—

⌐ANTONIO⌐ Ha, ha, ha.

⌐SEBASTIAN⌐ So. You're paid.

ADRIAN Uninhabitable and almost inaccessible— 40

SEBASTIAN Yet—

ADRIAN Yet—

ANTONIO He could not miss 't.

ADRIAN It must needs be of subtle, tender, and delicate temperance. 45

ANTONIO Temperance was a delicate wench.

SEBASTIAN Ay, and a subtle, as he most learnedly
delivered.

ADRIAN The air breathes upon us here most sweetly.

SEBASTIAN As if it had lungs, and rotten ones. 50

ANTONIO Or as 'twere perfumed by a fen.

GONZALO Here is everything advantageous to life.

ANTONIO True, save means to live.

SEBASTIAN Of that there's none, or little.

GONZALO How lush and lusty the grass looks! How 55
green!

ANTONIO The ground indeed is tawny.

SEBASTIAN With an eye of green in 't.

61. **rarity:** exceptional quality (Sebastian's comment pretends that the word here carries its meaning of "unusual occurrences" **vouched** [line 63] for by travelers.)

70. **pocket up:** conceal, suppress (with a pun on *pocket*)

72. **Afric:** i.e., Africa

76. **return:** i.e., journey home

78. **to:** i.e., as

79. **widow Dido: Dido,** queen of Carthage (See longer note, page 174.)

80. **A pox o':** i.e., curses on

85. **study of:** wonder about

90. **miraculous harp:** used by the mythological character Amphion to raise the walls of Thebes (Antonio and Sebastian say that Gonzalo's words have restored not only the walls but an entire city, Carthage.)

Amphion raising the walls of Thebes. (2.1.90–91)
From Flavius Philostratus, *Les images ou tableaux . . .* (1629).

ANTONIO   He misses not much.

SEBASTIAN   No, he doth but mistake the truth totally.   60

GONZALO   But the rarity of it is, which is indeed almost beyond credit—

SEBASTIAN   As many vouched rarities are.

GONZALO   That our garments, being, as they were, drenched in the sea, hold notwithstanding their   65 freshness and ⌈gloss,⌉ being rather new-dyed than stained with salt water.

ANTONIO   If but one of his pockets could speak, would it not say he lies?

SEBASTIAN   Ay, or very falsely pocket up his report.   70

GONZALO   Methinks our garments are now as fresh as when we put them on first in Afric, at the marriage of the King's fair daughter Claribel to the King of Tunis.

SEBASTIAN   'Twas a sweet marriage, and we prosper   75 well in our return.

ADRIAN   Tunis was never graced before with such a paragon to their queen.

GONZALO   Not since widow Dido's time.

ANTONIO   Widow? A pox o' that! How came that "wid-   80 ow" in? Widow Dido!

SEBASTIAN   What if he had said "widower Aeneas" too? Good Lord, how you take it!

ADRIAN, ⌈*to Gonzalo*⌉   "Widow Dido," said you? You make me study of that. She was of Carthage, not of   85 Tunis.

GONZALO   This Tunis, sir, was Carthage.

ADRIAN   Carthage?

GONZALO   I assure you, Carthage.

ANTONIO   His word is more than the miraculous harp.   90

SEBASTIAN   He hath raised the wall, and houses too.

ANTONIO   What impossible matter will he make easy next?

95. **his son:** i.e., to **his son**

96. **kernels:** i.e., seeds

99. **in good time:** an expression of ironical agreement (responding to Gonzalo's "Ay")

105. **Bate:** i.e., except for (literally, subtract)

107. **doublet:** short, close-fitting jacket

108. **in a sort:** i.e., in a way

109. **sort:** lot (in the drawing of lots)

113. **stomach:** desire, inclination; **sense:** perhaps, feelings

115. **rate:** estimation

116. **removed:** separated by space

121. **surges:** waves

123. **breasted:** confronted boldly

126. **lusty:** vigorous

127. **that . . . basis bowed:** i.e., that bent down over its (i.e., the shore's) eroded base

"The old cock." (2.1.32)
From Konrad Gesner, *Historiae animalium* . . . (1585–1604).

SEBASTIAN I think he will carry this island home in his
  pocket and give it his son for an apple. 95
ANTONIO And sowing the kernels of it in the sea, bring
  forth more islands.
GONZALO Ay.
ANTONIO Why, in good time.
GONZALO, ⌜*to Alonso*⌝ Sir, we were talking that our 100
  garments seem now as fresh as when we were at
  Tunis at the marriage of your daughter, who is now
  queen.
ANTONIO And the rarest that e'er came there.
SEBASTIAN Bate, I beseech you, widow Dido. 105
ANTONIO O, widow Dido? Ay, widow Dido.
GONZALO, ⌜*to Alonso*⌝ Is not, sir, my doublet as fresh as
  the first day I wore it? I mean, in a sort.
ANTONIO That "sort" was well fished for.
GONZALO, ⌜*to Alonso*⌝ When I wore it at your daughter's 110
  marriage.
ALONSO
  You cram these words into mine ears against
  The stomach of my sense. Would I had never
  Married my daughter there, for coming thence
  My son is lost, and, in my rate, she too, 115
  Who is so far from Italy removed
  I ne'er again shall see her.—O, thou mine heir
  Of Naples and of Milan, what strange fish
  Hath made his meal on thee?
FRANCISCO   Sir, he may live. 120
  I saw him beat the surges under him
  And ride upon their backs. He trod the water,
  Whose enmity he flung aside, and breasted
  The surge most swoll'n that met him. His bold head
  'Bove the contentious waves he kept, and oared 125
  Himself with his good arms in lusty stroke
  To th' shore, that o'er his wave-worn basis bowed,

128. **As:** i.e., **as** if it were

134. **at least:** i.e., **at** the **least**

135. **hath . . . on 't:** i.e., has reason to weep with grief over Claribel's banishment   **on 't:** i.e., of it

137. **importuned:** pronounced "impòrtuned"; **otherwise:** i.e., to act **otherwise**

139. **Weighed:** balanced; **loathness and obedience:** i.e., disinclination to her marriage **and obedience** to her father

140. **should bow:** i.e., she **should bow**

146. **dear'st:** i.e., most precious (or bitterest) part

149. **time:** the appropriate **time**

150. **plaster:** medicated bandage

152. **chirurgeonly:** i.e., like a surgeon

154. **cloudy:** i.e., darkened by grief; gloomy

157. **Had I plantation of:** i.e., if I were in charge of colonizing (Antonio responds as if by **plantation** Gonzalo had meant "to plant.")

As stooping to relieve him. I not doubt
He came alive to land.

ALONSO   No, no, he's gone.   130

SEBASTIAN
Sir, you may thank yourself for this great loss,
That would not bless our Europe with your daughter,
But rather lose her to an African,
Where she at least is banished from your eye,
Who hath cause to wet the grief on 't.   135

ALONSO   Prithee, peace.

SEBASTIAN
You were kneeled to and importuned otherwise
By all of us; and the fair soul herself
Weighed between loathness and obedience at
Which end o' th' beam should bow. We have lost   140
  your son,
I fear, forever. Milan and Naples have
More widows in them of this business' making
Than we bring men to comfort them.
The fault's your own.   145

ALONSO   So is the dear'st o' th' loss.

GONZALO   My lord Sebastian,
The truth you speak doth lack some gentleness
And time to speak it in. You rub the sore
When you should bring the plaster.   150

SEBASTIAN   Very well.

ANTONIO   And most chirurgeonly.

GONZALO, ⌜*to Alonso*⌝
It is foul weather in us all, good sir,
When you are cloudy.

SEBASTIAN   Foul weather?   155

ANTONIO   Very foul.

GONZALO
Had I plantation of this isle, my lord—

ANTONIO
He'd sow 't with nettle seed.

159. **docks:** a variety of coarse, weedy herb (See picture, page 66.) **mallows:** a variety of wild plant with hairy stems and leaves

160. **on 't:** i.e., of the island

161. **want:** lack

162–71, 175–80. **I' th' commonwealth . . . people:** See longer note, page 174.

162. **by contraries:** i.e., in a way opposite to what is customary

163. **traffic:** commerce

165. **Letters:** literature; learning, study

166. **use of service:** i.e., employment or other use of servants; **succession:** inheritance

167. **Bourn, bound of land:** Both terms mean "boundary." **tilth:** farm work

168. **corn:** i.e., wheat

169. **occupation:** mechanical or mercantile employment; handicraft; trade

175. **in common:** i.e., to be shared **in common**

177. **engine:** military weapon

179. **foison:** plenty, profusion

182. **idle:** worthless, lazy (an echo of line 169, where **idle** means "not occupied in work")

184. **the Golden Age:** In Greek mythology (as recounted in Book 1 of Ovid's *Metamorphoses*), the first **age** of man was **golden:** laws were not needed, nor was military power; food was abundant without human labor; spring lasted all the year; milk and wine ran in streams, and honey flowed from trees. (See picture, page 74.)

185. **'Save:** i.e., God save

187. **do you mark:** i.e., are you listening to

SEBASTIAN   Or docks, or mallows.
GONZALO
  And were the king on 't, what would I do?   160
SEBASTIAN   Scape being drunk, for want of wine.
GONZALO
  I' th' commonwealth I would by contraries
  Execute all things, for no kind of traffic
  Would I admit; no name of magistrate;
  Letters should not be known; riches, poverty,   165
  And use of service, none; contract, succession,
  Bourn, bound of land, tilth, vineyard, none;
  No use of metal, corn, or wine, or oil;
  No occupation; all men idle, all,
  And women too, but innocent and pure;   170
  No sovereignty—
SEBASTIAN   Yet he would be king on 't.
ANTONIO   The latter end of his commonwealth forgets
    the beginning.
GONZALO
  All things in common nature should produce   175
  Without sweat or endeavor; treason, felony,
  Sword, pike, knife, gun, or need of any engine
  Would I not have; but nature should bring forth
  Of its own kind all foison, all abundance,
  To feed my innocent people.   180
SEBASTIAN   No marrying 'mong his subjects?
ANTONIO   None, man, all idle: whores and knaves.
GONZALO
  I would with such perfection govern, sir,
  T' excel the Golden Age.
SEBASTIAN   'Save his Majesty!   185
ANTONIO
  Long live Gonzalo!
GONZALO   And do you mark me, sir?
ALONSO
  Prithee, no more. Thou dost talk nothing to me.

190. **minister occasion:** provide an opportunity (for laughter)

191. **sensible:** sensitive; **they . . . use:** i.e., it is their custom

198. **An:** if; **flatlong:** harmlessly (literally, with the flat of the sword)

199. **mettle:** spirit

200. **moon . . . sphere:** In Ptolemaic astronomy, the moon, like the sun and the planets, was thought to travel around the Earth in its own crystalline sphere. (See picture, page xxxii.)

202. **a-batfowling:** bird catching at night using long poles called "bats" with which to beat the trees in which the birds roost

204. **warrant you:** promise, guarantee; **adventure:** risk

205. **discretion:** i.e., reputation as a person of good judgment

206. **heavy:** sleepy

212. **omit:** disregard, fail to accept; **heavy:** weighty (also, sleepy)

GONZALO   I do well believe your Highness, and did it to
minister occasion to these gentlemen, who are of   190
such sensible and nimble lungs that they always use
to laugh at nothing.

ANTONIO   'Twas you we laughed at.

GONZALO   Who in this kind of merry fooling am
nothing to you. So you may continue, and laugh at   195
nothing still.

ANTONIO   What a blow was there given!

SEBASTIAN   An it had not fallen flatlong.

GONZALO   You are gentlemen of brave mettle. You
would lift the moon out of her sphere if she would   200
continue in it five weeks without changing.

   Enter Ariel ⌜invisible,⌝ playing solemn music.

SEBASTIAN   We would so, and then go a-batfowling.

ANTONIO, ⌜*to Gonzalo*⌝   Nay, good my lord, be not angry.

GONZALO   No, I warrant you, I will not adventure my
discretion so weakly. Will you laugh me asleep?   205
For I am very heavy.

ANTONIO   Go sleep, and hear us.
       ⌜*All sink down asleep except Alonso, Antonio,*
                  and Sebastian.⌝

ALONSO
What, all so soon asleep? I wish mine eyes
Would, with themselves, shut up my thoughts. I find
They are inclined to do so.   210

SEBASTIAN   Please you, sir,
Do not omit the heavy offer of it.
It seldom visits sorrow; when it doth,
It is a comforter.

ANTONIO   We two, my lord,   215
Will guard your person while you take your rest,
And watch your safety.

ALONSO   Thank you. Wondrous heavy.
             ⌜*Alonso sleeps. Ariel exits.*⌝

222. **sink:** i.e., close

225. **They:** i.e., all the others; **consent:** agreement

226. **as by a thunderstroke:** i.e., as if struck by lightning

229. **Th' occasion speaks thee:** i.e., the present opportunity **speaks** to you (or, perhaps, **speaks** your name)

232. **waking:** i.e., awake

235. **sleepy language: language** appropriate to sleep (and therefore, perhaps, fantastic, dreamlike)

241. **wink'st:** i.e., (you) close your eyes

243. **distinctly:** clearly, unambiguously

245. **than my custom:** i.e., than I ordinarily am

246. **if heed me:** i.e., **if** you pay attention to **me**

247. **Trebles thee o'er:** i.e., increases you threefold

248. **standing water:** i.e., patiently waiting (literally, still or stagnant **water,** the image that Antonio picks up in his response)

249. **flow:** advance (like the tide moving in)

Docks. (2.1.159)
From John Gerard, *The herball . . .* (1597).

SEBASTIAN
  What a strange drowsiness possesses them!
ANTONIO
  It is the quality o' th' climate. 220
SEBASTIAN   Why
  Doth it not then our eyelids sink? I find
  Not myself disposed to sleep.
ANTONIO   Nor I. My spirits are nimble.
  They fell together all, as by consent. 225
  They dropped as by a thunderstroke. What might,
  Worthy Sebastian, O, what might—? No more.
  And yet methinks I see it in thy face
  What thou shouldst be. Th' occasion speaks thee, and
  My strong imagination sees a crown 230
  Dropping upon thy head.
SEBASTIAN   What, art thou waking?
ANTONIO
  Do you not hear me speak?
SEBASTIAN   I do, and surely
  It is a sleepy language, and thou speak'st 235
  Out of thy sleep. What is it thou didst say?
  This is a strange repose, to be asleep
  With eyes wide open—standing, speaking, moving—
  And yet so fast asleep.
ANTONIO   Noble Sebastian, 240
  Thou let'st thy fortune sleep, die rather, wink'st
  Whiles thou art waking.
SEBASTIAN   Thou dost snore distinctly.
  There's meaning in thy snores.
ANTONIO
  I am more serious than my custom. You 245
  Must be so too, if heed me; which to do
  Trebles thee o'er.
SEBASTIAN   Well, I am standing water.
ANTONIO
  I'll teach you how to flow.

250. **ebb:** recede (like an ebb tide)

253. **purpose:** subject of discussion; **cherish:** foster, entertain

255. **invest:** clothe

256. **the bottom:** i.e., the ocean floor

257. **By:** because of

259. **The setting . . . cheek:** i.e., your expression

260. **A matter:** i.e., something important

261. **throes . . . yield:** i.e., causes you great suffering in delivery

263. **remembrance:** memory

264. **be of as little memory:** i.e., **be as little** remembered; or, have just **as little** memory

265. **earthed:** buried

266–67. **only . . . persuade:** i.e., makes counseling (or giving advice) his only profession

270. **hope:** expectation (Antonio picks up the word in its sense of hopeful anticipation.)

273. **that way:** i.e., with regard to Ferdinand's survival

275. **a wink:** i.e., the slightest bit; **beyond:** i.e., higher (than achieving the crown)

276. **But doubt discovery there:** perhaps, fears that it will (not) discover what it seeks even **there** (The language is very confused here, perhaps to indicate the intensity of Antonio's feelings or perhaps through scribal or printer error.)

283. **beyond man's life:** i.e., further than a man could travel in a lifetime

284. **note:** information; **post:** the messenger

SEBASTIAN   Do so. To ebb   250
  Hereditary sloth instructs me.
ANTONIO   O,
  If you but knew how you the purpose cherish
  Whiles thus you mock it, how in stripping it
  You more invest it. Ebbing men indeed   255
  Most often do so near the bottom run
  By their own fear or sloth.
SEBASTIAN   Prithee, say on.
  The setting of thine eye and cheek proclaim
  A matter from thee, and a birth indeed   260
  Which throes thee much to yield.
ANTONIO   Thus, sir:
  Although this lord of weak remembrance—this,
  Who shall be of as little memory
  When he is earthed—hath here almost persuaded—   265
  For he's a spirit of persuasion, only
  Professes to persuade—the King his son's alive,
  'Tis as impossible that he's undrowned
  As he that sleeps here swims.
SEBASTIAN   I have no hope   270
  That he's undrowned.
ANTONIO   O, out of that no hope
  What great hope have you! No hope that way is
  Another way so high a hope that even
  Ambition cannot pierce a wink beyond,   275
  But doubt discovery there. Will you grant with me
  That Ferdinand is drowned?
SEBASTIAN   He's gone.
ANTONIO   Then tell me,
  Who's the next heir of Naples?   280
SEBASTIAN   Claribel.
ANTONIO
  She that is Queen of Tunis; she that dwells
  Ten leagues beyond man's life; she that from Naples
  Can have no note, unless the sun were post—

286. **razorable:** i.e., bearded; **from whom:** perhaps, coming away **from whom**

287. **cast again:** vomited back up

288. **to perform an act:** i.e., were given an action to carry out (with a theatrical sense picked up in the word **prologue** in the following line)

289. **what to come:** i.e., that which is **to come**

295. **cubit:** an ancient measure of length (about 20 inches)

297. **us:** i.e., we cubits; **Keep:** stay (addressed to Claribel)

299–300. **they were . . . are:** a conventional equation of sleep and death

300. **There be that:** i.e., **there** are those who

303. **make:** i.e., be

304. **chough:** chattering crow (pronounced "chuff"); **deep chat:** i.e., meaningful talk

308. **content:** liking, pleasure

309. **Tender:** regard

314. **feater:** more becomingly or elegantly

315. **fellows:** companions; **men:** servants

316. **for:** as for (i.e., what about)

317. **kibe:** a sore on the heel resulting from exposure to the cold

318. **put . . . slipper:** i.e., force me to wear slippers

The man i' th' moon's too slow—till newborn chins 285
Be rough and razorable; she that from whom
We all were sea-swallowed, though some cast again,
And by that destiny to perform an act
Whereof what's past is prologue, what to come
In yours and my discharge. 290

SEBASTIAN What stuff is this? How say you?
  'Tis true my brother's daughter's Queen of Tunis,
  So is she heir of Naples, 'twixt which regions
  There is some space.

ANTONIO   A space whose ev'ry cubit 295
  Seems to cry out "How shall that Claribel
  Measure us back to Naples? Keep in Tunis
  And let Sebastian wake." Say this were death
  That now hath seized them, why, they were no worse
  Than now they are. There be that can rule Naples 300
  As well as he that sleeps, lords that can prate
  As amply and unnecessarily
  As this Gonzalo. I myself could make
  A chough of as deep chat. O, that you bore
  The mind that I do, what a sleep were this 305
  For your advancement! Do you understand me?

SEBASTIAN
  Methinks I do.

ANTONIO   And how does your content
  Tender your own good fortune?

SEBASTIAN   I remember 310
  You did supplant your brother Prospero.

ANTONIO   True,
  And look how well my garments sit upon me,
  Much feater than before. My brother's servants
  Were then my fellows; now they are my men. 315

SEBASTIAN But, for your conscience?

ANTONIO
  Ay, sir, where lies that? If 'twere a kibe,
  'Twould put me to my slipper, but I feel not

319. **This deity:** i.e., conscience

320. **Milan:** i.e., the dukedom of **Milan; candied:** congealed, frozen

321. **molest:** cause (me) trouble

325. **doing thus:** i.e., stabbing (The words may be accompanied by a stabbing gesture.)

326. **perpetual wink:** eternal sleep; **for aye:** forever

328. **Should not:** i.e., **should not** be allowed to; **course:** i.e., **course** of action

329. **take suggestion:** listen to persuasion

330. **tell the clock to:** perhaps, say it is the right time for

335. **tribute:** See 1.2.134 and 148.

338. **rear:** raise; **the like:** the same

339. **fall it:** let **it fall**

340 SD. **invisible:** i.e., **invisible** to the other characters

341. **art:** magic power

343. **them:** i.e., Alonso and Gonzalo (The use of **them** suggests that, in delivering these lines, Ariel turns from Gonzalo to the audience.)

346. **His:** its

347. **keep:** i.e., have

This deity in my bosom. Twenty consciences
That stand 'twixt me and Milan, candied be they   320
And melt ere they molest! Here lies your brother,
No better than the earth he lies upon.
If he were that which now he's like—that's dead—
Whom I with this obedient steel, three inches of it,
Can lay to bed forever; whiles you, doing thus,   325
To the perpetual wink for aye might put
This ancient morsel, this Sir Prudence, who
Should not upbraid our course. For all the rest,
They'll take suggestion as a cat laps milk.
They'll tell the clock to any business that   330
We say befits the hour.

SEBASTIAN   Thy case, dear friend,
Shall be my precedent: as thou got'st Milan,
I'll come by Naples. Draw thy sword. One stroke
Shall free thee from the tribute which thou payest,   335
And I the King shall love thee.

ANTONIO   Draw together,
And when I rear my hand, do you the like
To fall it on Gonzalo.   ⌜*They draw their swords.*⌝

SEBASTIAN   O, but one word.   340
                        ⌜*They talk apart.*⌝

Enter Ariel, ⌜*invisible,*⌝ *with music and song.*

ARIEL, ⌜*to the sleeping Gonzalo*⌝
My master through his art foresees the danger
That you, his friend, are in, and sends me forth—
For else his project dies—to keep them living.
Sings in Gonzalo's ear:
            While you here do snoring lie,
            Open-eyed conspiracy   345
                His time doth take.
            If of life you keep a care,
            Shake off slumber and beware.
                Awake, awake!

356. **securing:** guarding, keeping safe
365. **humming:** i.e., Ariel's song
369. **verily:** certain
370. **quit:** leave

A sixteenth-century image of the Golden Age. (2.1.184)
From Ovid, *Accípe studiose lector . . . Metamorphosin . . .* (1509).

ANTONIO, ⌐*to Sebastian*⌐ Then let us both be sudden. 350
GONZALO, ⌐*waking*⌐ Now, good angels preserve the
    King! ⌐*He wakes Alonso.*⌐
ALONSO, ⌐*to Sebastian*⌐
  Why, how now, ho! Awake? Why are you drawn?
  Wherefore this ghastly looking?
GONZALO, ⌐*to Sebastian*⌐ What's the matter? 355
SEBASTIAN
  Whiles we stood here securing your repose,
  Even now, we heard a hollow burst of bellowing
  Like bulls, or rather lions. Did 't not wake you?
  It struck mine ear most terribly.
ALONSO   I heard nothing. 360
ANTONIO
  O, 'twas a din to fright a monster's ear,
  To make an earthquake. Sure, it was the roar
  Of a whole herd of lions.
ALONSO   Heard you this, Gonzalo?
GONZALO
  Upon mine honor, sir, I heard a humming, 365
  And that a strange one too, which did awake me.
  I shaked you, sir, and cried. As mine eyes opened,
  I saw their weapons drawn. There was a noise,
  That's verily. 'Tis best we stand upon our guard,
  Or that we quit this place. Let's draw our weapons. 370
ALONSO
  Lead off this ground, and let's make further search
  For my poor son.
GONZALO   Heavens keep him from these beasts,
  For he is, sure, i' th' island.
ALONSO   Lead away. 375
ARIEL, ⌐*aside*⌐
  Prospero my lord shall know what I have done.
  So, king, go safely on to seek thy son.
                          They exit.

2.2 Having escaped the apparently sinking ship, Trinculo finds Caliban hiding under a cloak, under which Trinculo also crawls to take shelter from the storm. Stephano, drunk, finds them both and shares his bottle with them. In return, Caliban abandons Prospero's service and swears to be Stephano's subject.

---

2. **flats:** swamps, marshes; **Prosper:** i.e., Prospero

3. **By inchmeal:** inch by inch, little by little

4. **needs must:** i.e., **must; nor:** neither; **pinch:** See longer note to 1.2.392, page 173.

5. **urchin-shows:** i.e., apparitions of goblins

6. **like a firebrand in the dark:** i.e., as if they were an *ignis fatuus*, a phosphorescent light that hovers over swampy ground at night

9. **mow:** grimace, make faces

10. **after:** i.e., afterward

13. **wound:** i.e., **wound** about

15. **Here comes a spirit:** i.e., Trinculo, just entering

17. **mind:** notice

18. **bear off:** repel, ward off

21. **foul:** dirty; **bombard:** leather jug for holding liquor

22. **his:** i.e., its

24. **fall:** i.e., rain

27–28. **poor-John:** dried fish

Scene 2

Enter Caliban with a burden of wood. A noise of
thunder heard.

CALIBAN
All the infections that the sun sucks up
From bogs, fens, flats, on Prosper fall and make him
By inchmeal a disease! His spirits hear me,
And yet I needs must curse. But they'll nor pinch,
Fright me with urchin-shows, pitch me i' th' mire,   5
Nor lead me like a firebrand in the dark
Out of my way, unless he bid 'em. But
For every trifle are they set upon me,
Sometimes like apes, that mow and chatter at me
And after bite me; then like hedgehogs, which   10
Lie tumbling in my barefoot way and mount
Their pricks at my footfall. Sometime am I
All wound with adders, who with cloven tongues
Do hiss me into madness. Lo, now, lo!
Here comes a spirit of his, and to torment me   15
For bringing wood in slowly. I'll fall flat.
Perchance he will not mind me.
⌜*He lies down and covers himself with a cloak.*⌝

Enter Trinculo.

TRINCULO Here's neither bush nor shrub to bear off
any weather at all. And another storm brewing; I
hear it sing i' th' wind. Yond same black cloud, yond   20
huge one, looks like a foul bombard that would shed
his liquor. If it should thunder as it did before, I
know not where to hide my head. Yond same cloud
cannot choose but fall by pailfuls. ⌜*Noticing Cali-*
ban.⌝ What have we here, a man or a fish? Dead or   25
alive? A fish, he smells like a fish—a very ancient
and fishlike smell, a kind of not-of-the-newest poor-
John. A strange fish. Were I in England now, as once

29. **painted:** his picture **painted** and hung on a pole, as for a fair or sideshow (See *Macbeth* 5.8.29–30 and longer note, page 174.)

29–30. **not a . . . would:** i.e., every **fool** on **a holiday there would**

31. **make a man:** (1) **make** its owner's fortune; (2) be the equivalent of an Englishman

32. **doit:** tiny coin

34. **dead Indian:** See longer note to 2.2.29.

35. **o' my troth:** i.e., by my faith

37. **thunderbolt:** i.e., the supposed bolt or dart thought to cause the destruction when lightning strikes

39. **gaberdine:** cloak

41. **shroud:** take shelter

42. **dregs:** i.e., last drops of liquor (See **bombard** at line 21, above.)

42 SD. **crawls under:** We learn at lines 93–94 that Trinculo and Caliban are under the cloak facing in opposite directions, with Trinculo's head at Caliban's feet.

47. **swabber:** sailor who swabs the decks

51. **a tongue with a tang:** i.e., a sharp **tongue**

53. **tar, pitch:** associated with ships and sailors

57. **Do not torment me:** addressed to Trinculo, who has crawled under Caliban's cloak and whose frightened trembling Caliban misinterprets (See lines 81–83, below.)

I was, and had but this fish painted, not a holiday
fool there but would give a piece of silver. There   30
would this monster make a man. Any strange beast
there makes a man. When they will not give a doit to
relieve a lame beggar, they will lay out ten to see a
dead Indian. Legged like a man, and his fins like
arms! Warm, o' my troth! I do now let loose my   35
opinion, hold it no longer: this is no fish, but an
islander that hath lately suffered by a thunderbolt.
⌜*Thunder.*⌝ Alas, the storm is come again. My best
way is to creep under his gaberdine. There is no
other shelter hereabout. Misery acquaints a man   40
with strange bedfellows. I will here shroud till the
dregs of the storm be past.

     ⌜*He crawls under Caliban's cloak.*⌝

   Enter Stephano singing.

STEPHANO
    I shall no more to sea, to sea.
    Here shall I die ashore—
This is a very scurvy tune to sing at a man's funeral.   45
Well, here's my comfort.   *Drinks.*
Sings.
The master, the swabber, the boatswain, and I,
 The gunner and his mate,
Loved Mall, Meg, and Marian, and Margery,
 But none of us cared for Kate.   50
  For she had a tongue with a tang,
  Would cry to a sailor "Go hang!"
She loved not the savor of tar nor of pitch,
Yet a tailor might scratch her where'er she did itch.
  Then to sea, boys, and let her go hang!   55
This is a scurvy tune too. But here's my comfort.
       Drinks.

CALIBAN Do not torment me! O!

58. **What's the matter?:** i.e., **what's** going on?

58–59. **Do you ... Ind:** See longer note, page 175. **put tricks upon 's:** perhaps, play **tricks** on (i.e., try to fool) us; **men of Ind:** perhaps, "Indians"

61. **proper:** handsome

62. **four legs:** The actual saying is "goes on two **legs.**"

63. **give ground:** retreat

64. **at':** i.e., at the

67. **ague:** fever that makes him shiver (pronounced "à-gue")

69. **for that:** i.e., **for** learning **our language; recover:** cure

71–72. **trod ... leather:** i.e., wore shoes   **neat's:** cow's

77. **afore:** before; **go near to:** very nearly

78–79. **I will ... much:** i.e., I'll **take** as **much** as I can get

79–80. **that hath him:** i.e., **that** gets **him** (from me)

85. **Here ... cat:** Proverbial: "Liquor **that will** make a **cat** speak."

88. **chaps:** jaws

92. **delicate:** ingenious

93. **forward:** See note to 42 SD, above.

STEPHANO　What's the matter? Have we devils here? Do you put tricks upon 's with savages and men of Ind? Ha? I have not scaped drowning to be afeard now 60 of your four legs, for it hath been said "As proper a man as ever went on four legs cannot make him give ground," and it shall be said so again while Stephano breathes at' nostrils.

CALIBAN　The spirit torments me. O! 65

STEPHANO　This is some monster of the isle with four legs, who hath got, as I take it, an ague. Where the devil should he learn our language? I will give him some relief, if it be but for that. If I can recover him and keep him tame and get to Naples with him, 70 he's a present for any emperor that ever trod on neat's leather.

CALIBAN　Do not torment me, prithee. I'll bring my wood home faster.

STEPHANO　He's in his fit now, and does not talk after 75 the wisest. He shall taste of my bottle. If he have never drunk wine afore, it will go near to remove his fit. If I can recover him and keep him tame, I will not take too much for him. He shall pay for him that hath him, and that soundly. 80

CALIBAN　Thou dost me yet but little hurt. Thou wilt anon; I know it by thy trembling. Now Prosper works upon thee.

STEPHANO　Come on your ways. Open your mouth. Here is that which will give language to you, cat. 85 Open your mouth. This will shake your shaking, I can tell you, and that soundly. ⌜*Caliban drinks.*⌝ You cannot tell who's your friend. Open your chaps again.

TRINCULO　I should know that voice. It should be—but 90 he is drowned, and these are devils. O, defend me!

STEPHANO　Four legs and two voices—a most delicate monster! His forward voice now is to speak well of his friend. His backward voice is to utter foul

95–96. **If . . . will:** i.e., even if it takes . . . to

97. **Amen:** Stephano's response to Caliban's hearty drink

100. **call me:** i.e., **call me** by my name

102. **long spoon:** Proverbial: "He must have a **long spoon** that eats with the **devil.**"

110. **siege:** excrement; **mooncalf:** monster (whose deformity is blamed on the influence of the moon)

111. **vent:** excrete

112–13. **thunderstroke:** i.e., the impact of a stroke of lightning

115. **overblown:** i.e., blown over

119. **constant:** steady

120. **an if they be:** i.e., **if they** are

121. **sprites:** spirits; **brave:** splendid, admirable

125. **butt of sack:** barrel of sweet wine

126. **by this bottle:** i.e., swear **by this bottle**

127. **of the bark:** from, or out of, **the bark**

128. **since:** after

speeches and to detract. If all the wine in my bottle 95
will recover him, I will help his ague. Come.
⌜*Caliban drinks.*⌝ Amen! I will pour some in thy
other mouth.

TRINCULO Stephano!

STEPHANO Doth thy other mouth call me? Mercy, mer- 100
cy, this is a devil, and no monster! I will leave him; I
have no long spoon.

TRINCULO Stephano! If thou be'st Stephano, touch me
and speak to me, for I am Trinculo—be not
afeard—thy good friend Trinculo. 105

STEPHANO If thou be'st Trinculo, come forth. I'll pull
thee by the lesser legs. If any be Trinculo's legs,
these are they. ⌜*He pulls him out from under Caliban's cloak.*⌝ Thou art very Trinculo indeed. How
cam'st thou to be the siege of this mooncalf? Can 110
he vent Trinculos?

TRINCULO I took him to be killed with a thunderstroke. But art thou not drowned, Stephano? I
hope now thou art not drowned. Is the storm
overblown? I hid me under the dead mooncalf's 115
gaberdine for fear of the storm. And art thou living,
Stephano? O Stephano, two Neapolitans scaped!

STEPHANO Prithee, do not turn me about. My stomach
is not constant.

CALIBAN, ⌜*aside*⌝ These be fine things, an if they be not 120
sprites. That's a brave god and bears celestial liquor.
I will kneel to him.
⌜*He crawls out from under the cloak.*⌝

STEPHANO, ⌜*to Trinculo*⌝ How didst thou scape? How
cam'st thou hither? Swear by this bottle how thou
cam'st hither—I escaped upon a butt of sack, which 125
the sailors heaved o'erboard—by this bottle, which
I made of the bark of a tree with mine own hands,
since I was cast ashore.

135. **kiss the book:** i.e., take a drink (The allusion is to the practice of kissing the Bible before taking an oath.)

139. **cellar:** i.e., wine **cellar; rock:** See longer note to line 1.2.410, page 173.

144. **when time was:** i.e., once upon a **time**

146, 147. **dog, bush:** In legend, there is a man in the moon who carries a bundle of sticks or a **bush** and who is accompanied by a **dog.**

149. **anon:** soon

150. **By . . . light:** a mild oath; **shallow:** silly, trivial

153. **drawn:** i.e., drunk; **in good sooth:** a mild oath

157. **When 's:** i.e., **when** his

"Legged like a man, and his fins like arms." (2.2.34–35)
From Konrad Gesner, *Icones animalium quadrupedum* . . . (1560).

CALIBAN I'll swear upon that bottle to be thy true
subject, for the liquor is not earthly. 130

STEPHANO, ⌜*to Trinculo*⌝ Here. Swear then how thou
escapedst.

TRINCULO Swum ashore, man, like a duck. I can swim
like a duck, I'll be sworn.

STEPHANO Here, kiss the book. ⌜*Trinculo drinks.*⌝ 135
Though thou canst swim like a duck, thou art made
like a goose.

TRINCULO O Stephano, hast any more of this?

STEPHANO The whole butt, man. My cellar is in a rock
by th' seaside, where my wine is hid.—How now, 140
mooncalf, how does thine ague?

CALIBAN Hast thou not dropped from heaven?

STEPHANO Out o' th' moon, I do assure thee. I was the
man i' th' moon when time was.

CALIBAN I have seen thee in her, and I do adore thee. 145
My mistress showed me thee, and thy dog, and thy
bush.

STEPHANO Come, swear to that. Kiss the book. I will
furnish it anon with new contents. Swear.
⌜*Caliban drinks.*⌝

TRINCULO By this good light, this is a very shallow 150
monster. I afeard of him? A very weak monster. The
man i' th' moon? A most poor, credulous monster!
—Well drawn, monster, in good sooth!

CALIBAN I'll show thee every fertile inch o' th' island,
and I will kiss thy foot. I prithee, be my god. 155

TRINCULO By this light, a most perfidious and drunken
monster. When 's god's asleep, he'll rob his bottle.

CALIBAN I'll kiss thy foot. I'll swear myself thy subject.

STEPHANO Come on, then. Down, and swear.
⌜*Caliban kneels.*⌝

TRINCULO I shall laugh myself to death at this puppy- 160
headed monster. A most scurvy monster. I could
find in my heart to beat him—

164. **in drink:** i.e., drunk

173. **where crabs grow:** perhaps, to trees bearing crab apples; or, perhaps, to shallow water **where crabs** live

174. **pignuts:** earthnuts (edible legumes)

176. **marmoset:** small monkey

177. **filberts:** hazelnuts

178. **scamels:** This word is otherwise unknown. It may be a misprint for *sea mel*, i.e., a sea mew (a bird mentioned in travel literature of the time, considered a delicacy).

181. **else:** i.e., except us; **inherit:** take possession

183. **him:** i.e., it; **by and by:** soon

187. **firing:** i.e., firewood

189. **trenchering:** i.e., trenchers (wooden boards or plates on which food is served)

191. **man:** servant

192. **high-day:** A **high day** was a day of high or solemn celebration.

194. **brave:** splendid

STEPHANO Come, kiss.
TRINCULO —but that the poor monster's in drink. An
abominable monster. 165
CALIBAN
I'll show thee the best springs. I'll pluck thee berries.
I'll fish for thee and get thee wood enough.
A plague upon the tyrant that I serve.
I'll bear him no more sticks, but follow thee,
Thou wondrous man. 170
TRINCULO A most ridiculous monster, to make a won-
der of a poor drunkard.
CALIBAN, ⌈*standing*⌉
I prithee, let me bring thee where crabs grow.
And I with my long nails will dig thee pignuts,
Show thee a jay's nest, and instruct thee how 175
To snare the nimble marmoset. I'll bring thee
To clustering filberts, and sometimes I'll get thee
Young scamels from the rock. Wilt thou go with me?
STEPHANO I prithee now, lead the way without any
more talking.—Trinculo, the King and all our 180
company else being drowned, we will inherit here.
—Here, bear my bottle.—Fellow Trinculo, we'll
fill him by and by again.
CALIBAN *sings drunkenly*
        Farewell, master, farewell, farewell.
TRINCULO A howling monster, a drunken monster. 185
CALIBAN ⌈*sings*⌉
        No more dams I'll make for fish,
            Nor fetch in firing
            At requiring,
        Nor scrape trenchering, nor wash dish.
            'Ban, 'ban, Ca-caliban
            Has a new master. Get a new man. 190
        Freedom, high-day! High-day, freedom! Freedom,
        high-day, freedom!
STEPHANO O brave monster! Lead the way.
                                    They exit.

THE TEMPEST

ACT 3

3.1 Ferdinand is visited by Miranda. Prospero observes them unseen as they exchange marriage vows and clasp hands.

---

1. **sports:** games

1–2. **their labor . . . sets off:** perhaps, enjoyment of the games does away with our awareness of the pain they cause; or, perhaps, the pain they cause **sets off** (i.e., displays, as against a dark background) the **delight** we find in the games

2. **baseness:** i.e., base (menial) activities

3. **undergone:** undertaken; endured; **most poor:** i.e., very **poor**

4. **mean:** lowly, menial

5. **heavy:** tedious

6. **which:** i.e., whom; **quickens:** brings to life

11. **sore injunction:** strict command

14. **Had never like:** i.e., **never had** such an; **executor:** person performing the task

16. **Most busiest when I do it:** This difficult line is printed in the Folio as "Most busie lest, when I doe it," and sometimes appears in editions as "Most busil'est when I do it." There is no agreement about what "busiest" (or "busil'est") modifies, nor about what "it" refers to.

18. **would:** wish

20. **this:** i.e., the log you are carrying

ACT 3

Scene 1
Enter Ferdinand bearing a log.

FERDINAND
There be some sports are painful, and their labor
Delight in them ⌜sets⌝ off; some kinds of baseness
Are nobly undergone; and most poor matters
Point to rich ends. This my mean task
Would be as heavy to me as odious, but   5
The mistress which I serve quickens what's dead
And makes my labors pleasures. O, she is
Ten times more gentle than her father's crabbed,
And he's composed of harshness. I must remove
Some thousands of these logs and pile them up,   10
Upon a sore injunction. My sweet mistress
Weeps when she sees me work, and says such
     baseness
Had never like executor. I forget;
But these sweet thoughts do even refresh my labors, 15
Most ⌜busiest⌝ when I do it.

Enter Miranda; and Prospero ⌜at a distance, unobserved.⌝

MIRANDA   Alas now, pray you,
Work not so hard. I would the lightning had
Burnt up those logs that you are enjoined to pile.
Pray, set it down and rest you. When this burns   20

21. **'Twill weep:** literally, resin will ooze from it
38. **worm:** a biblical way of describing a human, emphasizing mortal frailties; **infected:** Love is often described as a sickness.
39. **visitation:** visit
46. **hest:** command
47. **Admired:** a translation of the name **Miranda**
52. **diligent:** attentive; **several:** various
54. **With so full soul:** i.e., so totally
55. **owed:** owned

Venus and Cupid, "dove-drawn." (4.1.104)
From Joannes ab Indagine, *The book of palmestry* (1666).

'Twill weep for having wearied you. My father
Is hard at study. Pray now, rest yourself.
He's safe for these three hours.

FERDINAND   O most dear mistress,
The sun will set before I shall discharge   25
What I must strive to do.

MIRANDA   If you'll sit down,
I'll bear your logs the while. Pray, give me that.
I'll carry it to the pile.

FERDINAND   No, precious creature,   30
I had rather crack my sinews, break my back,
Than you should such dishonor undergo
While I sit lazy by.

MIRANDA   It would become me
As well as it does you, and I should do it   35
With much more ease, for my good will is to it,
And yours it is against.

PROSPERO, ⌜*aside*⌝   Poor worm, thou art infected.
This visitation shows it.

MIRANDA   You look wearily.   40

FERDINAND
No, noble mistress, 'tis fresh morning with me
When you are by at night. I do beseech you,
Chiefly that I might set it in my prayers,
What is your name?

MIRANDA   Miranda.—O my father,   45
I have broke your hest to say so!

FERDINAND   Admired Miranda!
Indeed the top of admiration, worth
What's dearest to the world! Full many a lady
I have eyed with best regard, and many a time   50
Th' harmony of their tongues hath into bondage
Brought my too diligent ear. For several virtues
Have I liked several women, never any
With so full soul but some defect in her
Did quarrel with the noblest grace she owed,   55

56. **put it to the foil:** i.e., defeat or overthrow it (A **foil** is a weapon used in fencing.)

61. **Save:** except; **glass:** looking **glass,** mirror

63. **How features are abroad:** i.e., what people look like elsewhere

64. **skilless:** ignorant; **modesty:** virginity

65. **dower:** i.e., dowry

68. **like of:** i.e., **like**

71. **condition:** rank

73. **I would, not so:** i.e., I wish it were **not so**

74. **wooden slavery:** i.e., being condemned to carry these logs; **suffer:** allow

75. **The flesh-fly:** i.e., a fly that lays its eggs in dead flesh; **blow:** i.e., corrupt by laying eggs in

82. **event:** outcome

83–84. **if hollowly . . . mischief:** i.e., **if I speak** insincerely, turn the **best** of my future to evil

And put it to the foil. But you, O you,
So perfect and so peerless, are created
Of every creature's best.

MIRANDA   I do not know
One of my sex, no woman's face remember,   60
Save, from my glass, mine own. Nor have I seen
More that I may call men than you, good friend,
And my dear father. How features are abroad
I am skilless of, but by my modesty,
The jewel in my dower, I would not wish   65
Any companion in the world but you,
Nor can imagination form a shape
Besides yourself to like of. But I prattle
Something too wildly, and my father's precepts
I therein do forget.   70

FERDINAND   I am in my condition
A prince, Miranda; I do think a king—
I would, not so!—and would no more endure
This wooden slavery than to suffer
The flesh-fly blow my mouth. Hear my soul speak: 75
The very instant that I saw you did
My heart fly to your service, there resides
To make me slave to it, and for your sake
Am I this patient log-man.

MIRANDA   Do you love me?   80

FERDINAND
O heaven, O Earth, bear witness to this sound,
And crown what I profess with kind event
If I speak true; if hollowly, invert
What best is boded me to mischief. I,
Beyond all limit of what else i' th' world,   85
Do love, prize, honor you.

MIRANDA   I am a fool
To weep at what I am glad of.

PROSPERO, ⌈*aside*⌉   Fair encounter

92. **Wherefore:** why

96. **want:** i.e., do without; **trifling:** i.e., a frivolous waste of time

100–108. **I am your wife ... heart in 't:** This exchange of vows, expressed as it is in the present tense, constituted a legal betrothal in Renaissance England. The clasping of hands, or "handfasting" (at line 108), was usually done publicly; but even done privately, the vows and handfasting made the contract a legal marriage.

101. **maid:** maidservant (also, virgin); **fellow:** companion, equal

104. **My mistress:** i.e., the woman that I love and serve; **thus humble:** Ferdinand may here bow or kneel.

106. **willing:** desirous

107. **As bondage e'er of freedom:** i.e., as the enslaved ever wished for liberty

108 SD. **clasping his hand:** See note to lines 100–108, above.

110. **A thousand thousand:** i.e., a million (farewells)

112. **withal:** i.e., with all this; with this (event)

Of two most rare affections. Heavens rain grace   90
On that which breeds between 'em!
FERDINAND   Wherefore
  weep you?
MIRANDA
  At mine unworthiness, that dare not offer
  What I desire to give, and much less take   95
  What I shall die to want. But this is trifling,
  And all the more it seeks to hide itself,
  The bigger bulk it shows. Hence, bashful cunning,
  And prompt me, plain and holy innocence.
  I am your wife if you will marry me.   100
  If not, I'll die your maid. To be your fellow
  You may deny me, but I'll be your servant
  Whether you will or no.
FERDINAND
  My mistress, dearest, and I thus humble ever.
MIRANDA
  My husband, then?   105
FERDINAND   Ay, with a heart as willing
  As bondage e'er of freedom. Here's my hand.
MIRANDA, ⌈*clasping his hand*⌉
  And mine, with my heart in 't. And now farewell
  Till half an hour hence.
FERDINAND   A thousand thousand.   110
                                      They exit.

PROSPERO
  So glad of this as they I cannot be,
  Who are surprised withal; but my rejoicing
  At nothing can be more. I'll to my book,
  For yet ere suppertime must I perform
  Much business appertaining.   115
                                      He exits.

3.2 Trinculo and Caliban quarrel, and Stephano takes Caliban's part. Ariel, invisible, imitates Trinculo's voice and accuses Caliban of lying, causing further trouble among the three. Caliban calls Prospero a tyrant and urges Stephano to kill Prospero and take Miranda as his consort. Stephano and Trinculo join Caliban in following the music that Ariel plays to lead them out of their way.

---

2. **out:** empty; **before:** i.e., before that

3. **bear up and board 'em:** a naval command that seems here to mean "drink up"

10. **set:** perhaps, closed; or, fixed; or, sunk out of sight

11, 12. **set:** placed

12. **brave:** fine, splendid

15. **recover:** reach

16. **by this light:** a mild oath

17. **standard:** standard-bearer, ensign

18. **list:** please

18–19. **standard:** upright timber or pole

21. **go:** walk

27–28. **in case:** ready, prepared

28. **justle:** jostle, shake

Scene 2
Enter Caliban, Stephano, and Trinculo.

STEPHANO, ⌐*to Trinculo*⌐ Tell not me. When the butt is
out, we will drink water; not a drop before. Therefore bear up and board 'em.—Servant monster,
drink to me.

TRINCULO Servant monster? The folly of this island!   5
They say there's but five upon this isle; we are three
of them. If th' other two be brained like us, the state
totters.

STEPHANO Drink, servant monster, when I bid thee.
Thy eyes are almost set in thy head.   10

⌐*Caliban drinks.*⌐

TRINCULO Where should they be set else? He were a
brave monster indeed if they were set in his tail.

STEPHANO My man-monster hath drowned his tongue
in sack. For my part, the sea cannot drown me. I
swam, ere I could recover the shore, five-and-thirty   15
leagues off and on, by this light.—Thou shalt be my
lieutenant, monster, or my standard.

TRINCULO Your lieutenant, if you list. He's no standard.

STEPHANO We'll not run, Monsieur Monster.   20

TRINCULO Nor go neither. But you'll lie like dogs, and
yet say nothing neither.

STEPHANO Mooncalf, speak once in thy life, if thou
be'st a good mooncalf.

CALIBAN How does thy Honor? Let me lick thy shoe. I'll   25
not serve him; he is not valiant.

TRINCULO Thou liest, most ignorant monster. I am in
case to justle a constable. Why, thou debauched
fish, thou! Was there ever man a coward that hath
drunk so much sack as I today? Wilt thou tell a   30
monstrous lie, being but half a fish and half a
monster?

36. **natural:** simpleton, idiot (with wordplay on monsters as "unnatural")

38. **keep . . . head:** proverbial

43. **suit:** request, petition

44. **Marry:** a mild oath (originally an oath: "by the Virgin Mary")

54. **by this hand:** a mild oath; **supplant:** get rid of; root out

57. **Mum . . . more:** Proverbial: "I will say nothing but **mum.**"

CALIBAN   Lo, how he mocks me! Wilt thou let him, my
lord?

TRINCULO   "Lord," quoth he? That a monster should be   35
such a natural!

CALIBAN   Lo, lo again! Bite him to death, I prithee.

STEPHANO   Trinculo, keep a good tongue in your head.
If you prove a mutineer, the next tree. The poor
monster's my subject, and he shall not suffer   40
indignity.

CALIBAN   I thank my noble lord. Wilt thou be pleased
to harken once again to the suit I made to thee?

STEPHANO   Marry, will I. Kneel and repeat it. I will
stand, and so shall Trinculo.   45

Enter Ariel, invisible.

CALIBAN, ⌜*kneeling*⌝   As I told thee before, I am subject
to a tyrant, a sorcerer, that by his cunning hath
cheated me of the island.

ARIEL, ⌜*in Trinculo's voice*⌝   Thou liest.

CALIBAN, ⌜*to Trinculo*⌝   Thou liest, thou jesting monkey,   50
thou. ⌜*He stands.*⌝ I would my valiant master would
destroy thee. I do not lie.

STEPHANO   Trinculo, if you trouble him any more in 's
tale, by this hand, I will supplant some of your
teeth.   55

TRINCULO   Why, I said nothing.

STEPHANO   Mum then, and no more. ⌜*Trinculo stands
aside.*⌝ Proceed.

CALIBAN

I say by sorcery he got this isle;

From me he got it. If thy Greatness will,   60

Revenge it on him, for I know thou dar'st,

But this thing dare not.

STEPHANO   That's most certain.

CALIBAN

Thou shalt be lord of it, and I'll serve thee.

70. **pied ninny, patch:** perhaps references to Trinculo's profession as a Fool (**ninny, patch**) and to the Fool's parti-colored (**pied**) clothing. (But see longer note, page 175.)

74. **quick:** flowing; **freshes:** streams of fresh water

78. **stockfish:** Proverbial: "To beat like a **stockfish**" (Dried cod, or *stock*, was beaten to make it tender before cooking.)

84. **give me the lie:** i.e., accuse me of lying

86, 87. **A pox o', A murrain on:** i.e., a plague on, curses on

91. **stand further off:** Some editors think this remark should be addressed to Caliban, and that it refers to his unpleasant odor.

A "pied ninny." (3.2.70)
From William Kemp, *Kempes nine daies wonder* . . .
(1600; 1884 facs.).

STEPHANO How now shall this be compassed? Canst 65
    thou bring me to the party?

CALIBAN
  Yea, yea, my lord. I'll yield him thee asleep,
  Where thou mayst knock a nail into his head.

ARIEL, ⌜*in Trinculo's voice*⌝ Thou liest. Thou canst not.

CALIBAN
  What a pied ninny's this!—Thou scurvy patch!— 70
  I do beseech thy Greatness, give him blows
  And take his bottle from him. When that's gone,
  He shall drink naught but brine, for I'll not show him
  Where the quick freshes are.

STEPHANO Trinculo, run into no further danger. Inter- 75
    rupt the monster one word further, and by this
    hand, I'll turn my mercy out o' doors and make a
    stockfish of thee.

TRINCULO Why, what did I? I did nothing. I'll go
    farther off. 80

STEPHANO Didst thou not say he lied?

ARIEL, ⌜*in Trinculo's voice*⌝ Thou liest.

STEPHANO Do I so? Take thou that. ⌜*He beats Trinculo.*⌝
    As you like this, give me the lie another time.

TRINCULO I did not give the lie! Out o' your wits and 85
    hearing too? A pox o' your bottle! This can sack and
    drinking do. A murrain on your monster, and the
    devil take your fingers!

CALIBAN Ha, ha, ha!

STEPHANO Now forward with your tale. ⌜*To Trinculo.*⌝ 90
    Prithee, stand further off.

CALIBAN
  Beat him enough. After a little time
  I'll beat him too.

STEPHANO Stand farther. ⌜*Trinculo moves farther
    away.*⌝ Come, proceed. 95

CALIBAN
  Why, as I told thee, 'tis a custom with him

97. **brain him:** smash in his skull

99. **paunch:** stab in the paunch or belly

100. **weasand:** windpipe

102. **sot:** fool, blockhead

104. **Burn but:** i.e., you must be sure to **burn** (or, perhaps, **burn** only)

105. **brave:** splendid; **utensils:** household goods (pronounced at the time "ùtensils")

106. **he'll deck withal:** i.e., **he'll** adorn (his house) with

109. **a nonpareil:** i.e., one without equal

113. **brave:** splendid

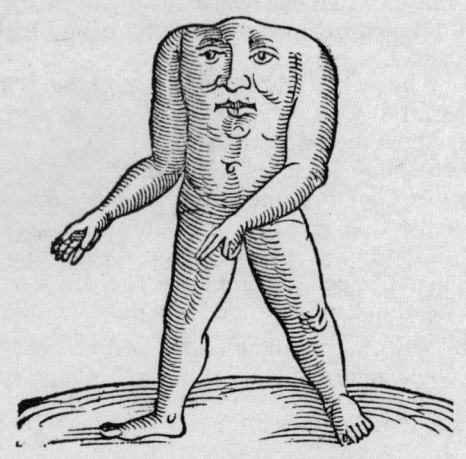

"Such men / Whose heads stood in their breasts."
(3.3.61–62)
From Conrad Lycosthenes, *Prodigiorum . . .* (1557).

I' th' afternoon to sleep. There thou mayst brain him,
Having first seized his books, or with a log
Batter his skull, or paunch him with a stake,
Or cut his weasand with thy knife. Remember 100
First to possess his books, for without them
He's but a sot, as I am, nor hath not
One spirit to command. They all do hate him
As rootedly as I. Burn but his books.
He has brave utensils—for so he calls them— 105
Which, when he has a house, he'll deck withal.
And that most deeply to consider is
The beauty of his daughter. He himself
Calls her a nonpareil. I never saw a woman
But only Sycorax my dam and she; 110
But she as far surpasseth Sycorax
As great'st does least.

STEPHANO   Is it so brave a lass?

CALIBAN
Ay, lord, she will become thy bed, I warrant,
And bring thee forth brave brood. 115

STEPHANO Monster, I will kill this man. His daughter
and I will be king and queen—save our Graces!—
and Trinculo and thyself shall be viceroys.—Dost
thou like the plot, Trinculo?

TRINCULO Excellent. 120

STEPHANO Give me thy hand. I am sorry I beat thee.
But while thou liv'st, keep a good tongue in thy
head.

CALIBAN
Within this half hour will he be asleep.
Wilt thou destroy him then? 125

STEPHANO   Ay, on mine honor.

ARIEL, ⌈*aside*⌉ This will I tell my master.

CALIBAN
Thou mak'st me merry. I am full of pleasure.

129. **troll:** sing; **catch:** music written for three voices, sung as a round

130. **but whilere:** just a little while ago

131. **reason:** what is reasonable

133. **cout:** a nonsense word to rhyme with **flout** and **scout** (i.e., mock)

135. **Thought is free:** proverbial

136 SD. **tabor:** small drum

142. **take 't as thou list:** Proverbial: "**Take** it **as** you **list**" and "The **devil take** it."

144. **He that dies pays all debts:** proverbial

149. **airs:** melodies

Playing a tabor and pipe. (3.2.136 SD)
From William Kemp, *Kempes nine daies wonder . . .*
(1600; 1884 facs.).

Let us be jocund. Will you troll the catch
You taught me but whilere? 130

STEPHANO At thy request, monster, I will do reason,
any reason.—Come on, Trinculo, let us sing.
Sings.

> *Flout 'em and cout 'em*
> *And scout 'em and flout 'em!*
> *Thought is free.* 135

CALIBAN That's not the tune.

> *Ariel plays the tune on a tabor and pipe.*

STEPHANO What is this same?

TRINCULO This is the tune of our catch played by the
picture of Nobody.

STEPHANO, ⌈*to the invisible musician*⌉ If thou be'st a 140
man, show thyself in thy likeness. If thou be'st a
devil, take 't as thou list.

TRINCULO O, forgive me my sins!

STEPHANO He that dies pays all debts.—I defy thee!—
Mercy upon us! 145

CALIBAN Art thou afeard?

STEPHANO No, monster, not I.

CALIBAN
Be not afeard. The isle is full of noises,
Sounds and sweet airs that give delight and hurt not.
Sometimes a thousand twangling instruments 150
Will hum about mine ears, and sometimes voices
That, if I then had waked after long sleep,
Will make me sleep again; and then, in dreaming,
The clouds methought would open, and show riches
Ready to drop upon me, that when I waked 155
I cried to dream again.

STEPHANO This will prove a brave kingdom to me,
where I shall have my music for nothing.

CALIBAN When Prospero is destroyed.

STEPHANO That shall be by and by. I remember the 160
story.

163. **after:** i.e., afterward

3.3 King Alonso and his party, weary with searching, are visited by "strange shapes" bringing in a banquet, while Prospero, unseen, observes them. But when Alonso and his party take up the shapes' invitation to eat and drink, Ariel appears as a Harpy and makes the food and drink vanish. The Harpy accuses Alonso, Sebastian, and Antonio of usurping Prospero's dukedom and threatens them with worse than death. The three "men of sin" leave in a desperate state.

---

1. **By 'r lakin:** a mild oath: "by the Virgin Mary" ("by our little Lady")

2. **a maze:** an intricate set of interconnecting paths that lead confusingly to (and away from) a center (See picture, page 166.)

3. **forthrights and meanders:** i.e., paths that go straight and those that wind

3–4. **By your patience:** a polite phrase requesting permission

7. **attached:** seized

8. **dulling:** i.e., enervation, wearying

12. **frustrate:** defeated; or, useless

13. **right:** very

14. **for one repulse:** i.e., because our action was driven back, repelled

17. **throughly:** thoroughly

19. **travel:** This word is spelled "trauaile" (i.e., travail) in the Folio, and it means both "travel" and "labor."

TRINCULO   The sound is going away. Let's follow it, and after do our work.
STEPHANO   Lead, monster. We'll follow.—I would I could see this taborer. He lays it on. Wilt come?   165
TRINCULO   I'll follow, Stephano.

They exit.

Scene 3
Enter Alonso, Sebastian, Antonio, Gonzalo, Adrian, Francisco, etc.

GONZALO
By 'r lakin, I can go no further, sir.
My old bones aches. Here's a maze trod indeed
Through forthrights and meanders. By your
   patience,
I needs must rest me.   5
ALONSO   Old lord, I cannot blame thee,
Who am myself attached with weariness
To th' dulling of my spirits. Sit down and rest.
Even here I will put off my hope and keep it
No longer for my flatterer. He is drowned   10
Whom thus we stray to find, and the sea mocks
Our frustrate search on land. Well, let him go.
ANTONIO, ⌜*aside to Sebastian*⌝
I am right glad that he's so out of hope.
Do not, for one repulse, forgo the purpose
That you resolved t' effect.   15
SEBASTIAN, ⌜*aside to Antonio*⌝   The next advantage
Will we take throughly.
ANTONIO, ⌜*aside to Sebastian*⌝   Let it be tonight;
For now they are oppressed with travel, they
Will not nor cannot use such vigilance   20
As when they are fresh.
SEBASTIAN, ⌜*aside to Antonio*⌝   I say tonight. No more.

22 SD, 24 SD, 50 SD. **Solemn . . . depart:** In the Folio, these directions appear as a single combined stage direction just after our line 21.

22 SD. **on the top:** i.e., on a level high above the stage; **invisible:** perhaps, not seen by the characters onstage; or perhaps wearing a garment that signaled his invisibility (See note to 1.2.451 SD.)

24 SD. **banquet:** sumptuous food and drink

25. **keepers:** guardian angels

26. **living:** animate; **drollery:** comic play; puppet show; drawing, caricature

28. **phoenix:** a mythical bird that consumes itself in fire every 500 years and rises again from the ashes (See picture, page 160.)

31. **what does else want credit:** i.e., anything else that is incredible (Both Sebastian and Antonio, in lines 26–33, are alluding to travelers' tales and the unbelievable things they report.)

37. **certes:** certainly

39. **gentle:** courteous

45. **muse:** wonder at

48. **want:** lack

49. **dumb discourse:** silent language

Solemn and strange music, and ⌐enter⌐ Prospero on the top invisible.

ALONSO
What harmony is this? My good friends, hark.
GONZALO Marvelous sweet music!

Enter several strange shapes, bringing in a banquet, and dance about it with gentle actions of salutations.

ALONSO
Give us kind keepers, heavens! What were these? 25
SEBASTIAN
A living drollery! Now I will believe
That there are unicorns, that in Arabia
There is one tree, the phoenix' throne, one phoenix
At this hour reigning there.
ANTONIO   I'll believe both; 30
And what does else want credit, come to me
And I'll be sworn 'tis true. Travelers ne'er did lie,
Though fools at home condemn 'em.
GONZALO   If in Naples
I should report this now, would they believe me? 35
If I should say I saw such ⌐islanders⌐—
For, certes, these are people of the island—
Who, though they are of monstrous shape, yet note
Their manners are more gentle, kind, than of
Our human generation you shall find 40
Many, nay, almost any.
PROSPERO, ⌐*aside*⌐   Honest lord,
Thou hast said well, for some of you there present
Are worse than devils.
ALONSO   I cannot too much muse 45
Such shapes, such gesture, and such sound, expressing—
Although they want the use of tongue—a kind
Of excellent dumb discourse.

50. **Praise in departing:** Proverbial: "Save your compliments until the visit is ended."

53. **viands:** food and drink

54. **stomachs:** appetites

57–65. **When . . . warrant of:** more allusions to incredible travelers' tales

58. **mountaineers:** mountain people

59. **Dewlapped:** i.e., with folds of skin under their necks

61. **Wallets:** protuberances, wattles

62. **heads stood in their breasts:** See picture, page 104.

64–65. **Each . . . warrant of:** i.e., every traveler will guarantee to be true (See longer note, page 175.)

66. **stand to:** set to work; begin eating

67. **Although my last:** i.e., even though this might be **my last** meal

68. **best:** i.e., best part of my life

69 SD. **like a Harpy:** in the guise of a **Harpy,** a mythological creature with the face and breasts of a woman and the wings and talons of a bird (See picture, page 116, and longer note, page 175.) **a quaint device:** a theatrical machine that makes the food disappear from the table

71. **to instrument:** i.e., as its instrument

76. **such-like valor:** i.e., the courage of madness, of desperation

PROSPERO, ⌜*aside*⌝   Praise in departing.   50
    Inviting the King, etc., to eat, ⌜*the shapes*⌝ *depart.*

FRANCISCO   They vanished strangely.

SEBASTIAN   No matter, since
  They have left their viands behind, for we have
    stomachs.
  Will 't please you taste of what is here?   55

ALONSO   Not I.

GONZALO
  Faith, sir, you need not fear. When we were boys,
  Who would believe that there were mountaineers
  Dewlapped like bulls, whose throats had hanging at
    'em   60
  Wallets of flesh? Or that there were such men
  Whose heads stood in their breasts? Which now we
    find
  Each putter-out of five for one will bring us
  Good warrant of.   65

ALONSO   I will stand to and feed.
  Although my last, no matter, since I feel
  The best is past. Brother, my lord the Duke,
  Stand to, and do as we.
             ⌜*Alonso, Sebastian, and Antonio*
                    move toward the table.⌝

Thunder and lightning. Enter Ariel, like a Harpy, claps
his wings upon the table, and with a quaint device the
             banquet vanishes.

ARIEL ⌜*as Harpy*⌝
  You are three men of sin, whom Destiny,   70
  That hath to instrument this lower world
  And what is in 't, the never-surfeited sea
  Hath caused to belch up you, and on this island,
  Where man doth not inhabit, you 'mongst men
  Being most unfit to live. I have made you mad;   75
  And even with such-like valor, men hang and drown

77. **Their proper selves:** i.e., themselves

78. **I and my fellows:** In the harpy stories on which this scene is modeled, there are always three harpies. It is possible that other harpies appear with Ariel. (See line 69 SD.)

80. **whom:** i.e., which; **as well:** i.e., just as easily

82. **still-closing:** i.e., always coming back together (after being stabbed)

83. **dowl:** tiny feather; **fellow ministers:** See note to line 78.

84. **like:** likewise; **could hurt:** i.e., had the power to wound us

85. **massy:** massive

86. **uplifted:** i.e., picked up, lifted

89. **requit it:** i.e., avenged their exposure

95. **perdition:** utter destruction, ruin (The word also carries its theological sense of the fate of those in hell, the unredeemed.)

97. **ways:** paths; **whose wraths:** i.e., the fury of the powers

101. **clear:** pure, innocent

101 SD. **mocks and mows:** mocking gestures and grimaces

102. **Bravely:** splendidly

103. **devouring:** Perhaps when the food disappeared, it looked as if the Harpy had devoured it; or, perhaps, the word describes Ariel's engrossing performance or its effect on the "men of sin."

104. **bated:** omitted

105. **So:** i.e., in the same way; **with good life:** i.e., in a lifelike way

106. **observation:** i.e., attention to detail; **strange:** wonderful; **my meaner ministers:** the lesser agents of my plot, the other spirits

Their proper selves.
⌜*Alonso, Sebastian, and Antonio draw their swords.*⌝
          You fools, I and my fellows
Are ministers of Fate. The elements
Of whom your swords are tempered may as well   80
Wound the loud winds or with bemocked-at stabs
Kill the still-closing waters as diminish
One dowl that's in my plume. My fellow ministers
Are like invulnerable. If you could hurt,
Your swords are now too massy for your strengths   85
And will not be uplifted. But remember—
For that's my business to you—that you three
From Milan did supplant good Prospero,
Exposed unto the sea, which hath requit it,
Him and his innocent child, for which foul deed,   90
The powers—delaying, not forgetting—have
Incensed the seas and shores, yea, all the creatures
Against your peace. Thee of thy son, Alonso,
They have bereft; and do pronounce by me
Ling'ring perdition, worse than any death   95
Can be at once, shall step by step attend
You and your ways, whose wraths to guard you
    from—
Which here, in this most desolate isle, else falls
Upon your heads—is nothing but heart's sorrow   100
And a clear life ensuing.   *He vanishes in thunder.*

Then, to soft music, enter the shapes again, and dance,
  with mocks and mows, and carrying out the table.

PROSPERO, ⌜*aside*⌝
Bravely the figure of this Harpy hast thou
Performed, my Ariel. A grace it had, devouring.
Of my instruction hast thou nothing bated
In what thou hadst to say. So, with good life   105
And observation strange, my meaner ministers

107. **Their several kinds have done:** To "do one's kind" is to act according to one's nature.

117–20. **Methought . . . my trespass:** Alonso describes the harpy's speech as having come to his ears like the sounds of waves, wind, and thunder. **bass my trespass:** (1) provide a bass accompaniment to the singing of the wind; (2) intone my sin in bass notes; (3) proclaim the baseness of my actions

121. **Therefor:** because of that trespass

124–25. **But . . . o'er:** i.e., **I'll fight legions** of fiends if they appear **one at a time** (See longer note, page 175.)

126. **second:** support, backup

131. **ecstasy:** madness

A Harpy. (3.3.69 SD)
From Conrad Lycosthenes, *Prodigiorum . . .* (1557).

Their several kinds have done. My high charms
   work,
And these mine enemies are all knit up
In their distractions. They now are in my power;   110
And in these fits I leave them while I visit
Young Ferdinand, whom they suppose is drowned,
And his and mine loved darling.   ⌈*He exits, above.*⌉

GONZALO, ⌈*to Alonso*⌉
I' th' name of something holy, sir, why stand you
In this strange stare?   115

ALONSO   O, it is monstrous, monstrous!
Methought the billows spoke and told me of it;
The winds did sing it to me, and the thunder,
That deep and dreadful organ pipe, pronounced
The name of Prosper. It did bass my trespass.   120
Therefor my son i' th' ooze is bedded, and
I'll seek him deeper than e'er plummet sounded,
And with him there lie mudded.   *He exits.*

SEBASTIAN   But one fiend at a time,
I'll fight their legions o'er.   125

ANTONIO   I'll be thy second.
    They exit.

GONZALO
All three of them are desperate. Their great guilt,
Like poison given to work a great time after,
Now 'gins to bite the spirits. I do beseech you
That are of suppler joints, follow them swiftly   130
And hinder them from what this ecstasy
May now provoke them to.

ADRIAN   Follow, I pray you.
    They all exit.

THE TEMPEST

ACT 4

4.1 Prospero releases Ferdinand and gives him Miranda as his bride-to-be. To celebrate the prospect of their union, Prospero instructs Ariel to have the spirits under Prospero's control perform a masque. During the masque, Prospero remembers the threat posed by Caliban and stops the masque. He joins Ariel in driving off Caliban, Stephano, and Trinculo with spirits in the guise of dogs.

---

1. **austerely:** harshly

3. **a third of mine own life:** There has been much speculation about this phrase. Prospero may mean simply that Miranda is a large part of his **life.**

4. **Or:** i.e., in other words; **who:** i.e., whom

5. **tender:** present, offer

7. **strangely:** wonderfully; **afore:** before

11. **halt:** limp

13. **Against an oracle:** i.e., even if a deity should reveal the contrary through **an oracle**

16–20. **If . . . grow:** Even though, in Renaissance England, the exchange of vows and the handfasting in 3.1 were enough legally to marry Miranda and Ferdinand, Prospero speaks for the church when he says that a happy, prosperous marriage will not follow if the couple engages in sexual relations before the marriage is blessed with a sacred ceremony.

17. **sanctimonious:** sacred

19. **aspersion:** dew

20. **grow:** prosper (But the word also carries forward the image of the marriage as a seedbed on which heaven may drop dew or in which horrible **weeds** [line 22] may grow.)

ACT 4

Scene 1
Enter Prospero, Ferdinand, and Miranda.

PROSPERO, ⌈*to Ferdinand*⌉
  If I have too austerely punished you,
  Your compensation makes amends, for I
  Have given you here a third of mine own life,
  Or that for which I live; who once again
  I tender to thy hand. All thy vexations   5
  Were but my trials of thy love, and thou
  Hast strangely stood the test. Here afore heaven
  I ratify this my rich gift. O Ferdinand,
  Do not smile at me that I boast ⌈of her,⌉
  For thou shalt find she will outstrip all praise   10
  And make it halt behind her.
FERDINAND   I do believe it
  Against an oracle.
PROSPERO
  Then, as my ⌈gift⌉ and thine own acquisition
  Worthily purchased, take my daughter. But   15
  If thou dost break her virgin-knot before
  All sanctimonious ceremonies may
  With full and holy rite be ministered,
  No sweet aspersion shall the heavens let fall
  To make this contract grow; but barren hate,   20
  Sour-eyed disdain, and discord shall bestrew

24. **Hymen's lamps:** i.e., torches carried in a wedding procession (Hymen, the god of marriage, is often depicted with a torch in his hand. See picture, page 170.)

28. **opportune:** pronounced "oppòrtune"; **suggestion:** temptation

29. **Our worser genius:** i.e., our evil attendant spirit; **can:** i.e., **can** give (**Can** also had the meaning of "know," a meaning that may be included here.)

31. **that day's celebration:** i.e., the day our marriage is formally celebrated

32–33. **When I ... below:** i.e., **when I shall think night** will never come **or:** either **Phoebus' steeds:** i.e., the horses that pull the sun across the sky (Phoebus is the mythological god of the sun.) **are foundered:** have broken down

36. **What:** an interjection, here suggesting impatience

38. **meaner fellows:** lesser spirits

40. **trick:** i.e., performance; **rabble:** i.e., the **meaner fellows**

44. **vanity:** trifle; **of mine art:** i.e., that displays my magic powers

46. **Presently:** immediately

47. **with a twink:** i.e., "in the twinkling of an eye"

51. **mop and mow:** grimaces

The union of your bed with weeds so loathly
That you shall hate it both. Therefore take heed,
As Hymen's lamps shall light you.

FERDINAND   As I hope   25
For quiet days, fair issue, and long life,
With such love as 'tis now, the murkiest den,
The most opportune place, the strong'st suggestion
Our worser genius can shall never melt
Mine honor into lust to take away   30
The edge of that day's celebration
When I shall think or Phoebus' steeds are foundered
Or night kept chained below.

PROSPERO   Fairly spoke.
Sit then and talk with her. She is thine own.   35
⌜*Ferdinand and Miranda move aside.*⌝
What, Ariel, my industrious servant, Ariel!

Enter Ariel.

ARIEL
What would my potent master? Here I am.

PROSPERO
Thou and thy meaner fellows your last service
Did worthily perform, and I must use you
In such another trick. Go bring the rabble,   40
O'er whom I give thee power, here to this place.
Incite them to quick motion, for I must
Bestow upon the eyes of this young couple
Some vanity of mine art. It is my promise,
And they expect it from me.   45

ARIEL   Presently?

PROSPERO   Ay, with a twink.

ARIEL
        Before you can say "Come" and "Go,"
        And breathe twice, and cry "So, so,"
        Each one, tripping on his toe,   50
        Will be here with mop and mow.
        Do you love me, master? No?

55. **conceive:** understand

56. **true:** steadfast, honorable

56–57. **give . . . the rein:** allow . . . too free motion **dalliance:** amorous behavior

59. **goodnight:** i.e., farewell to

61–62. **The . . . liver:** Ferdinand here rephrases his promise that his honor will not melt into lust. The **liver** was thought to be the seat of the passions.

64. **corollary:** i.e., an unneeded extra

65. **want:** lack, need; **pertly:** quickly, nimbly

66. **No tongue:** i.e., no speaking

66 SD. **Enter Iris:** Iris's entrance begins the wedding masque. (See longer note, page 176.)

67. **Ceres:** goddess of the earth (Ceres does not enter until asked to approach at line 83. See picture, page 128.)

67–78. **thy rich leas . . . air:** Iris lists the kinds of earth over which Ceres reigns (**leas, mountains, meads, banks, groves, vineyard,** and **sea marge**), all of which Juno will ask Ceres to **leave** (line 80).

67. **leas:** fields

68. **vetches:** weedy plants grown for fodder

70. **thatched with stover:** covered with forage; **them to keep:** i.e., to feed the sheep

71. **pionèd and twillèd brims:** This much-debated phrase may describe the earth (trenched and protected with a mat of vegetation against erosion), or **pionèd** may describe flowers (i.e., "peonied").

72. **hest:** command

73. **cold:** i.e., chaste

74. **broom groves:** clumps of shrubs

75. **dismissèd:** i.e., discarded (by his sweetheart)

76. **Being lass-lorn:** having lost his lass; **poll-clipped:** i.e., pruned   *(continued)*

PROSPERO
Dearly, my delicate Ariel. Do not approach
Till thou dost hear me call.

ARIEL   Well; I conceive.   55
He exits.

PROSPERO, ⌈*to Ferdinand*⌉
Look thou be true; do not give dalliance
Too much the rein. The strongest oaths are straw
To th' fire i' th' blood. Be more abstemious,
Or else goodnight your vow.

FERDINAND   I warrant you, sir,   60
The white cold virgin snow upon my heart
Abates the ardor of my liver.

PROSPERO   Well.—
Now come, my Ariel. Bring a corollary
Rather than want a spirit. Appear, and pertly.   65
Soft music.
No tongue. All eyes. Be silent.

Enter Iris.

IRIS
Ceres, most bounteous lady, thy rich leas
Of wheat, rye, barley, vetches, oats, and peas;
Thy turfy mountains, where live nibbling sheep,
And flat meads thatched with stover, them to keep;   70
Thy banks with pionèd and twillèd brims,
Which spongy April at thy hest betrims
To make cold nymphs chaste crowns; and thy
    broom groves,
Whose shadow the dismissèd bachelor loves,   75
Being lass-lorn; thy poll-clipped vineyard,
And thy sea marge, sterile and rocky hard,
Where thou thyself dost air—the Queen o' th' sky,
Whose wat'ry arch and messenger am I,
Bids thee leave these, and with her sovereign grace,   80
Here on this grass-plot, in this very place,

77. **marge:** margin, beach

78. **Queen o' th' sky:** Juno, **queen** of the gods

79. **wat'ry arch:** i.e., rainbow (See picture, page 130.)

80. **these:** i.e., the territories ruled by Ceres

80–82. **with her sovereign grace . . . come and sport:** i.e., **come and sport . . . with** Juno

82. **peacocks:** sacred to Juno; **amain:** in haste

85. **wife of Jupiter:** i.e., Juno **Jupiter:** king of the gods

89. **bosky:** bush-covered; **unshrubbed down:** treeless uplands

90. **Rich scarf:** i.e., Iris, the rainbow

93–94. **estate / On:** i.e., give to

96. **Venus, her son:** i.e., the goddess of love and **her son,** Cupid

97. **attend:** accompany; or, serve as attendants for

97–98. **they did plot . . . got:** Dis (god of the underworld) abducted Ceres' daughter to be his bride. (See longer note, page 176.)

99. **her blind boy:** Cupid, depicted as blindfolded to show that "love is blind"; **scandaled:** scandalous

103. **Paphos:** a city in Cyprus devoted to Venus

104. **Dove-drawn:** Venus is often represented in a chariot drawn by doves. (See picture, page 92.)

106. **wanton:** lewd

108. **Hymen's . . . lighted:** i.e., the marriage formally celebrated (See note to 4.1.24.) **in vain:** i.e., Venus's plan to put a **charm** [line 106] on Miranda and Ferdinand has come to nothing

109. **Mars's hot minion:** i.e., Venus, lover of Mars, the god of war

(continued)

To come and sport. ⌜Her⌝ peacocks fly amain.
Approach, rich Ceres, her to entertain.

Enter Ceres.

CERES
  Hail, many-colored messenger, that ne'er
  Dost disobey the wife of Jupiter;   85
  Who with thy saffron wings upon my flowers
  Diffusest honey drops, refreshing showers;
  And with each end of thy blue bow dost crown
  My bosky acres and my unshrubbed down,
  Rich scarf to my proud Earth. Why hath thy queen 90
  Summoned me hither to this short-grassed green?
IRIS
  A contract of true love to celebrate,
  And some donation freely to estate
  On the blest lovers.
CERES   Tell me, heavenly bow, 95
  If Venus or her son, as thou dost know,
  Do now attend the Queen? Since they did plot
  The means that dusky Dis my daughter got,
  Her and her blind boy's scandaled company
  I have forsworn.   100
IRIS   Of her society
  Be not afraid. I met her deity
  Cutting the clouds towards Paphos, and her son
  Dove-drawn with her. Here thought they to have
    done   105
  Some wanton charm upon this man and maid,
  Whose vows are that no bed-right shall be paid
  Till Hymen's torch be lighted—but in vain.
  Mars's hot minion is returned again;
  Her waspish-headed son has broke his arrows, 110
  Swears he will shoot no more, but play with
    sparrows,
  And be a boy right out.

110. **waspish-headed:** irritable, hotheaded; **arrows:** Cupid's **arrows** cause his victims to fall in love.

113. **right out:** i.e., outright

113 SD. **Juno descends:** In the Folio, the descent of Juno is marked in the margin opposite lines 80–81. Some editors have argued that Juno should slowly descend from that moment until she speaks at line 116.

114–15. **Highest . . . comes:** i.e., **Juno, highest queen of state, comes**

118. **issue:** offspring

123. **foison:** abundance

124. **garners:** granaries

127–28. **Spring . . . harvest:** i.e., may **spring** join to **the very end of** autumn (so that there is no winter)

138. **wise:** See longer note, page 176.

Ceres. (4.1.67)
From Cesare Ripa, *Iconologia . . .* (1613).

Juno descends.

CERES   Highest queen of state,
Great Juno, comes. I know her by her gait.   115
JUNO
How does my bounteous sister? Go with me
To bless this twain, that they may prosperous be
And honored in their issue.
They sing.
JUNO

Honor, riches, marriage-blessing,
Long continuance and increasing,   120
Hourly joys be still upon you.
Juno sings her blessings on you.

⌜CERES⌝

Earth's increase, foison plenty,
Barns and garners never empty,
Vines with clust'ring bunches growing,   125
Plants with goodly burden bowing;
Spring come to you at the farthest
In the very end of harvest.
Scarcity and want shall shun you.
Ceres' blessing so is on you.   130

FERDINAND
This is a most majestic vision, and
Harmonious charmingly. May I be bold
To think these spirits?
PROSPERO   Spirits, which by mine art
I have from their confines called to enact   135
My present fancies.
FERDINAND   Let me live here ever.
So rare a wondered father and a wise
Makes this place paradise.

Juno and Ceres whisper,
and send Iris on employment.
PROSPERO   Sweet now, silence.   140

143. **our spell:** i.e., the magic **spell** controlling the masque

144. **naiads:** water nymphs; **windring:** This word may be a cross between *wandering* and *winding*.

145. **sedged crowns:** garlands made of sedge (a river plant)

153–54. **encounter ... In country footing:** join ... **in a country** dance

154 SD, 158 SD. **Enter ... vanish:** In the Folio, these stage directions are combined into a single direction that appears at our 154 SD.

154 SD. **properly habited:** dressed appropriately

158. **Avoid:** depart

158 SD. **heavily:** perhaps, reluctantly

159. **passion:** deep emotion

160. **works:** affects, agitates

162. **distempered:** troubled, upset

163. **moved:** disturbed; **sort:** manner

Iris. (4.1.66 SD, 79)
From Natale Conti, *Mythologiae . . .* (1616).

Juno and Ceres whisper seriously.
There's something else to do. Hush, and be mute,
Or else our spell is marred.

IRIS
You nymphs, called naiads of the windring brooks,
With your sedged crowns and ever-harmless looks,　　145
Leave your crisp channels and on this green land
Answer your summons, Juno does command.
Come, temperate nymphs, and help to celebrate
A contract of true love. Be not too late.

Enter certain Nymphs.

You sunburned sicklemen, of August weary,　　150
Come hither from the furrow and be merry.
Make holiday: your rye-straw hats put on,
And these fresh nymphs encounter every one
In country footing.

Enter certain Reapers, properly habited. They join with
the Nymphs in a graceful dance, towards the end
whereof Prospero starts suddenly and speaks.

PROSPERO
I had forgot that foul conspiracy　　155
Of the beast Caliban and his confederates
Against my life. The minute of their plot
Is almost come.—Well done. Avoid. No more.
　　　　　　To a strange, hollow, and confused noise,
　　　　　　　　⌜*the spirits*⌝ *heavily vanish.*
FERDINAND, ⌜*to Miranda*⌝
This is strange. Your father's in some passion
That works him strongly.　　160
MIRANDA　　　　　　　Never till this day
Saw I him touched with anger, so distempered.
PROSPERO, ⌜*to Ferdinand*⌝
You do look, my son, in a moved sort,
As if you were dismayed. Be cheerful, sir.

165. **revels:** In the courts of Queen Elizabeth and of King James, **revels** were presented at special seasons and included plays and masques. (See longer note to 4.1.66 SD, page 176.)

166. **foretold you:** i.e., already explained to you

168. **baseless fabric:** i.e., structure with no foundation; **vision:** spectacle

170. **the great globe:** i.e., the Earth (but with a probable allusion to the **Globe** Theater)

171. **inherit:** own; inhabit, dwell in

173. **rack:** wisp of cloud; **stuff:** material, fabric

174. **on:** i.e., of

175. **rounded with:** surrounded by (or, perhaps, ended by)

180. **still:** quiet

186. **presented Ceres:** perhaps, produced the masque of **Ceres;** or, perhaps, acted the part of **Ceres**

189. **varlets:** rascals

Our revels now are ended. These our actors, 165
As I foretold you, were all spirits and
Are melted into air, into thin air;
And like the baseless fabric of this vision,
The cloud-capped towers, the gorgeous palaces,
The solemn temples, the great globe itself, 170
Yea, all which it inherit, shall dissolve,
And, like this insubstantial pageant faded,
Leave not a rack behind. We are such stuff
As dreams are made on, and our little life
Is rounded with a sleep. Sir, I am vexed. 175
Bear with my weakness. My old brain is troubled.
Be not disturbed with my infirmity.
If you be pleased, retire into my cell
And there repose. A turn or two I'll walk
To still my beating mind. 180

FERDINAND/MIRANDA   We wish your peace.
⌜*They*⌝ *exit.*

Enter Ariel.

PROSPERO
Come with a thought. I thank thee, Ariel. Come.
ARIEL
Thy thoughts I cleave to. What's thy pleasure?
PROSPERO   Spirit,
We must prepare to meet with Caliban. 185
ARIEL
Ay, my commander. When I presented Ceres,
I thought to have told thee of it, but I feared
Lest I might anger thee.
PROSPERO
Say again, where didst thou leave these varlets?
ARIEL
I told you, sir, they were red-hot with drinking, 190
So full of valor that they smote the air
For breathing in their faces, beat the ground

193. **bending:** inclining (i.e., moving)
195. **unbacked:** i.e., unbroken, never ridden
197. **Advanced:** lifted
198. **So I charmed:** i.e., **I so** enchanted
199. **lowing:** mooing
200. **furzes, gorse:** evergreen shrubs
209. **stale:** bait, lure
212. **Nurture:** education; moral training (Prospero in these lines uses the language of European "discoverers" who argued that it was futile to attempt to civilize "savages" through humane treatment or education.)
213. **taken:** i.e., undertaken
215. **cankers:** corrupts
216 SD. **glistering:** i.e., glittering, sparkling
217. **line:** linden (lime) tree
220. **fairy:** supernatural creature
222. **jack:** rascal

The "blind mole." (4.1.218)
From Edward Topsell, *The historie of foure-footed beastes . . .* (1607).

For kissing of their feet; yet always bending
Towards their project. Then I beat my tabor,
At which, like unbacked colts, they pricked their   195
    ears,
Advanced their eyelids, lifted up their noses
As they smelt music. So I charmed their ears
That, calf-like, they my lowing followed through
Toothed briers, sharp furzes, pricking gorse, and   200
    thorns,
Which entered their frail shins. At last I left them
I' th' filthy-mantled pool beyond your cell,
There dancing up to th' chins, that the foul lake
O'erstunk their feet.   205

PROSPERO   This was well done, my bird.
Thy shape invisible retain thou still.
The trumpery in my house, go bring it hither
For stale to catch these thieves.

ARIEL   I go, I go.   *He exits.* 210

PROSPERO
A devil, a born devil, on whose nature
Nurture can never stick; on whom my pains,
Humanely taken, all, all lost, quite lost;
And as with age his body uglier grows,
So his mind cankers. I will plague them all   215
Even to roaring.

Enter Ariel, loaden with glistering apparel, etc.

Come, hang ⌜them on⌝ this line.

*Enter Caliban, Stephano, and Trinculo, all wet, ⌜as
Prospero and Ariel look on.⌝*

CALIBAN Pray you, tread softly, that the blind mole
    may not hear a footfall. We now are near his cell.

STEPHANO Monster, your fairy, which you say is a   220
    harmless fairy, has done little better than played the
    jack with us.

227. **lost:** ruined, destroyed, damned

228. **favor:** i.e., goodwill

230. **hoodwink this mischance:** i.e., wipe out the unhappiness you speak of **hoodwink:** blindfold **mischance:** unhappy occurrence

242. **good mischief:** i.e., the murder of Prospero

244. **For aye:** forever

247–49. **O King . . . thee:** Trinculo here echoes a popular song that begins "**King** Stephen was a **worthy peer.**" The song is about old and new cloaks and other apparel. (One stanza of the song is sung in *Othello* 2.3.)

251–52. **a frippery:** a secondhand-clothing shop (Trinculo argues that he and Stephano can tell that the apparel on the lime tree is not cast-off clothing.)

A blindfold or "hoodwink." (4.1.230)
From Johann Mannich, *Sacra emblemata . . .* (1624).

TRINCULO   Monster, I do smell all horse piss, at which
my nose is in great indignation.

STEPHANO   So is mine.—Do you hear, monster. If I 225
should take a displeasure against you, look you—

TRINCULO   Thou wert but a lost monster.

CALIBAN
Good my lord, give me thy favor still.
Be patient, for the prize I'll bring thee to
Shall hoodwink this mischance. Therefore speak 230
   softly.
All's hushed as midnight yet.

TRINCULO   Ay, but to lose our bottles in the pool!

STEPHANO   There is not only disgrace and dishonor in
that, monster, but an infinite loss. 235

TRINCULO   That's more to me than my wetting. Yet this
is your harmless fairy, monster!

STEPHANO   I will fetch off my bottle, though I be o'er
ears for my labor.

CALIBAN
Prithee, my king, be quiet. Seest thou here, 240
This is the mouth o' th' cell. No noise, and enter.
Do that good mischief which may make this island
Thine own forever, and I, thy Caliban,
For aye thy foot-licker.

STEPHANO   Give me thy hand. I do begin to have bloody 245
thoughts.

TRINCULO, ⌜*seeing the apparel*⌝ O King Stephano, O
peer, O worthy Stephano, look what a wardrobe
here is for thee!

CALIBAN
Let it alone, thou fool. It is but trash. 250

TRINCULO   Oho, monster, we know what belongs to a
frippery. ⌜*He puts on one of the gowns.*⌝ O King
Stephano!

STEPHANO   Put off that gown, Trinculo. By this hand,
I'll have that gown. 255

257. **dropsy:** a disease in which fluid accumulates in the body

258. **luggage:** burdensome trash (literally, that which has to be lugged around)

260. **crown:** head; **pinches:** See longer note to 1.2.392, page 173.

262. **Mistress Line:** addressed to the linden tree

264–65. **Now . . . jerkin:** Stephano puns on **line:** The jacket is "**under the line**" in that it has been taken off the tree, but the phrase also means "on the equator" (i.e., in the tropics)—apparently a joke about sailors losing their hair from tropical diseases or syphilis. (The **jerkin** is presumably trimmed with fur.)

266. **Do, do:** an expression of approval; **We . . . level:** i.e., **we steal** in proper fashion (**By line and level** was proverbial; **level** refers to a carpenter's level and **line** means "plumb line"—another pun on "**line.**") **an 't like:** i.e., if it please

271. **pass of pate:** i.e., witty play on words (A **pass** is a sword thrust; the **pate** is the head or the brains.)

272. **lime:** i.e., birdlime (to make his fingers sticky)

275. **barnacles:** i.e., barnacle geese (thought to be hatched from **barnacles,** and thus considered freaks of nature)

276. **villainous:** i.e., villainously, miserably

277. **lay to:** i.e., use

279. **Go to:** an expression of impatience

281 SD. **divers:** several; **setting them on:** urging them to attack

282–84. **Mountain, Silver, Fury, Tyrant:** the names of the "dogs"

TRINCULO   Thy Grace shall have it.

CALIBAN
The dropsy drown this fool! What do you mean
To dote thus on such luggage? ⌜Let 't⌝ alone,
And do the murder first. If he awake,
From toe to crown he'll fill our skins with pinches,   260
Make us strange stuff.

STEPHANO   Be you quiet, monster.—Mistress Line, is
not this my jerkin? ⌜*He takes a jacket from the tree.*⌝
Now is the jerkin under the line.—Now, jerkin, you
are like to lose your hair and prove a bald jerkin.   265

TRINCULO   Do, do. We steal by line and level, an 't like
your Grace.

STEPHANO   I thank thee for that jest. Here's a garment
for 't. Wit shall not go unrewarded while I am king
of this country. "Steal by line and level" is an ex-   270
cellent pass of pate. There's another garment for 't.

TRINCULO   Monster, come, put some lime upon your
fingers, and away with the rest.

CALIBAN
I will have none on 't. We shall lose our time
And all be turned to barnacles or to apes   275
With foreheads villainous low.

STEPHANO   Monster, lay to your fingers. Help to bear
this away where my hogshead of wine is, or I'll turn
you out of my kingdom. Go to, carry this.

TRINCULO   And this.   280

STEPHANO   Ay, and this.

A noise of hunters heard.

Enter divers spirits in shape of dogs and hounds,
hunting them about, Prospero and Ariel setting them on.

PROSPERO   Hey, Mountain, hey!

ARIEL   Silver! There it goes, Silver!

PROSPERO
Fury, Fury! There, Tyrant, there! Hark, hark!
⌜*Caliban, Stephano, and Trinculo are driven off.*⌝

285. **charge . . . that they:** i.e., order **my goblins** to; **their joints:** i.e., the **joints** of Caliban, Stephano, and Trinculo

287. **pinch-spotted:** i.e., bruised

289. **pard:** i.e., leopard; **cat o' mountain:** i.e., catamount (any of various wild cats)

294. **a little:** i.e., **a little** while

A panther, or "cat o' mountain." (4.1.289)
From Edward Topsell, *The historie of foure-footed beastes . . .* (1607).

Go, charge my goblins that they grind their joints 285
With dry convulsions, shorten up their sinews
With agèd cramps, and more pinch-spotted make
  them
Than pard or cat o' mountain.
ARIEL   Hark, they roar. 290
PROSPERO
Let them be hunted soundly. At this hour
Lies at my mercy all mine enemies.
Shortly shall all my labors end, and thou
Shalt have the air at freedom. For a little
Follow and do me service. 295

                                        They exit.

THE TEMPEST

ACT 5

5.1 Prospero releases Alonso and the court party from their charmed state and renounces the further use of his magic. Alonso restores Prospero to the dukedom of Milan, and, in return, Prospero reunites him with Ferdinand. Ariel arrives with the ship's master and boatswain, and all are soon joined by Caliban, Stephano, and Trinculo, whom Prospero sends off to decorate his cell. As they prepare to set sail for Naples, Prospero gives Ariel his freedom.

1–2. **Now . . . crack not:** Prospero speaks here as if he were an alchemist transmuting base metal into gold. A *projection* was the transmutation of metals in a crucible. **project:** plan, scheme **gather to a head:** come to the critical point **crack not:** hold firm—with a possible reference to the cracking of a heated crucible

3. **his carriage:** its burden

4. **On:** approaching

8. **and 's:** i.e., and his

11. **gave in charge:** commanded

13. **line grove:** grove of linden trees; **weather-fends:** protects against bad weather

14. **till your release:** i.e., until you release them

15. **abide:** continue; **distracted:** crazed, troubled in mind

16. **the remainder:** i.e., the other courtiers

21. **eaves of reeds:** i.e., thatched roofs

21–22. **works 'em:** operates upon them

ACT 5

Scene 1
Enter Prospero in his magic robes, and Ariel.

PROSPERO
Now does my project gather to a head.
My charms crack not, my spirits obey, and time
Goes upright with his carriage.—How's the day?

ARIEL
On the sixth hour, at which time, my lord,
You said our work should cease. 5

PROSPERO   I did say so
When first I raised the tempest. Say, my spirit,
How fares the King and 's followers?

ARIEL   Confined
  together 10
In the same fashion as you gave in charge,
Just as you left them; all prisoners, sir,
In the line grove which weather-fends your cell.
They cannot budge till your release. The King,
His brother, and yours abide all three distracted, 15
And the remainder mourning over them,
Brimful of sorrow and dismay; but chiefly
Him that you termed, sir, the good old Lord
  Gonzalo.
His tears runs down his beard like winter's drops 20
From eaves of reeds. Your charm so strongly works
  'em

23. **affections:** feelings, disposition

28. **touch:** sense

30. **One of their kind:** i.e., human as they are

30–31. **that relish ... as they:** i.e., **that** experience suffering just **as** keenly **as they** do

31. **kindlier:** (1) more compassionately; (2) more like humankind

32. **high:** serious, grave; extreme

32–33. **th' quick:** tender, sensitive flesh ("To touch **to** the **quick**" means to cause great mental pain or irritation.)

34–35. **with ... part:** i.e., in the battle between **reason** and **fury,** I take the side of **reason,** which is **nobler** than anger

35. **The rarer action:** i.e., **action** that is seldom performed (See longer note, page 177.)

42–59. **You elves ... potent art:** See longer note, page 177.

42. **standing:** still

44. **Neptune:** god of the sea—here, the sea itself; **fly:** flee from

45. **demi-puppets:** half-sized or dwarf puppets

46. **green sour ringlets:** i.e., fairy rings (small circles of grass around toadstools)

47. **not bites:** i.e., does not eat

48. **midnight mushrumps:** i.e., mushrooms that spring up overnight

49. **curfew:** ringing of the evening bell

50. **Weak masters:** i.e., the **elves** and **demi-puppets** invoked by Prospero (See longer note, page 177.)

52. **azured vault:** sky

That if you now beheld them, your affections
Would become tender.

PROSPERO　　　　　　　　Dost thou think so, spirit?　　25

ARIEL
Mine would, sir, were I human.

PROSPERO　　　　　　　　And mine shall.
Hast thou, which art but air, a touch, a feeling
Of their afflictions, and shall not myself,
One of their kind, that relish all as sharply　　30
Passion as they, be kindlier moved than thou art?
Though with their high wrongs I am struck to th'
　　quick,
Yet with my nobler reason 'gainst my fury
Do I take part. The rarer action is　　35
In virtue than in vengeance. They being penitent,
The sole drift of my purpose doth extend
Not a frown further. Go, release them, Ariel.
My charms I'll break, their senses I'll restore,
And they shall be themselves.　　40

ARIEL　　　　　　　　I'll fetch them, sir.
　　　　　　　　　　　　　　He exits.

⌜*Prospero draws a large circle on the stage with his staff.*⌝

PROSPERO
You elves of hills, brooks, standing lakes, and groves,
And you that on the sands with printless foot
Do chase the ebbing Neptune, and do fly him
When he comes back; you demi-puppets that　　45
By moonshine do the green sour ringlets make,
Whereof the ewe not bites; and you whose pastime
Is to make midnight mushrumps, that rejoice
To hear the solemn curfew; by whose aid,
Weak masters though you be, I have bedimmed　　50
The noontide sun, called forth the mutinous winds,
And 'twixt the green sea and the azured vault

54. Have I given fire: perhaps, **I have** provided the lightning

54–55. rifted . . . bolt: i.e., split the oak tree with a thunderbolt (**Jove,** the Roman king of the gods, held the oak tree sacred; he is also known as the god who hurls the thunderbolt [that is, a discharge of lightning]. See picture, page 32.)

56. spurs: deep roots

58. their sleepers: i.e., the dead

59. potent art: powerful magic; **rough:** perhaps, violent; or, perhaps, unpolished, rude

60. required: summoned

62. work mine end: i.e., accomplish my purposes

63. airy charm: both called from the air and appearing as an "air" or melody; **staff:** magic wand

65. plummet: weight attached to the end of a plumb line; **sound:** sink into water to measure its depth

67–116. A solemn . . . country: Prospero and Ariel are not seen or heard by the other characters until Prospero addresses Alonso at line 117.

67. A solemn air: i.e., this **solemn** melody

69. boiled: seething

70. spell-stopped: i.e., controlled by my magic spell

72. sociable to: i.e., companionable with; **the show of thine:** i.e., the appearance of your (weeping) eyes

73. Fall fellowly drops: i.e., let **fall** sympathetic tears; **apace:** quickly

75. rising senses: i.e., their dawning awareness described as if it were the sun appearing above the horizon

(continued)

148

Set roaring war; to the dread rattling thunder
Have I given fire, and rifted Jove's stout oak
With his own bolt; the strong-based promontory   55
Have I made shake, and by the spurs plucked up
The pine and cedar; graves at my command
Have waked their sleepers, oped, and let 'em forth
By my so potent art. But this rough magic
I here abjure, and when I have required   60
Some heavenly music, which even now I do,
          ⌜*Prospero gestures with his staff.*⌝
To work mine end upon their senses that
This airy charm is for, I'll break my staff,
Bury it certain fathoms in the earth,
And deeper than did ever plummet sound   65
I'll drown my book.   *Solemn music.*

Here enters Ariel before; then Alonso with a frantic
gesture, attended by Gonzalo; Sebastian and Antonio in
like manner attended by Adrian and Francisco. They all
  enter the circle which Prospero had made, and there
    stand charmed; which Prospero observing, speaks.

A solemn air, and the best comforter
To an unsettled fancy, cure thy brains,
Now useless, ⌜boiled⌝ within thy skull. There stand,
For you are spell-stopped.—   70
Holy Gonzalo, honorable man,
Mine eyes, e'en sociable to the show of thine,
Fall fellowly drops.—The charm dissolves apace,
And as the morning steals upon the night,
Melting the darkness, so their rising senses   75
Begin to chase the ignorant fumes that mantle
Their clearer reason.—O good Gonzalo,
My true preserver and a loyal sir
To him thou follow'st, I will pay thy graces
Home, both in word and deed.—Most cruelly   80

76. **ignorant fumes:** i.e., **fumes** that keep them **ignorant** (i.e., unaware of their surroundings, unconscious)

78. **sir:** gentleman

79–80. **pay . . . Home:** i.e., reward . . . fully

82. **furtherer:** supporter

83. **pinched:** tormented

85. **entertained:** harbored, cherished

86. **remorse:** compassion, pity; **nature:** i.e., natural feeling; **whom:** i.e., who

87. **inward pinches:** See longer note to 1.2.392, page 173.

91. **reasonable shore:** i.e., the shoreline of their reason

95. **discase me:** i.e., remove the clothes I am now wearing

96. **was sometime Milan:** i.e., appeared formerly as duke of **Milan**

100. **couch:** lie

102. **After summer:** i.e., following **summer** from clime to clime

106. **So, so, so:** probably Prospero's indication that he is now properly attired

107. **To:** i.e., go to

109. **Under the hatches:** below deck

109–10. **The master . . . Being awake:** i.e., when you have waked **the master and the boatswain**

110. **enforce them:** drive them by force

111. **presently:** immediately

Didst thou, Alonso, use me and my daughter.
Thy brother was a furtherer in the act.—
Thou art pinched for 't now, Sebastian.—Flesh and
  blood,
You, brother mine, that ⌈entertained⌉ ambition,   85
Expelled remorse and nature, whom, with Sebastian,
Whose inward pinches therefore are most strong,
Would here have killed your king, I do forgive thee,
Unnatural though thou art.—Their understanding
Begins to swell, and the approaching tide   90
Will shortly fill the reasonable shore
That now ⌈lies⌉ foul and muddy. Not one of them
That yet looks on me, or would know me.—Ariel,
Fetch me the hat and rapier in my cell.
                ⌈*Ariel exits and at once returns*
                    with Prospero's ducal robes.⌉
I will discase me and myself present   95
As I was sometime Milan.—Quickly, spirit,
Thou shalt ere long be free.
ARIEL *sings, and helps to attire him.*

    Where the bee sucks, there suck I.
    In a cowslip's bell I lie.
    There I couch when owls do cry.   100
    On the bat's back I do fly
    After summer merrily.
  Merrily, merrily shall I live now
  Under the blossom that hangs on the bow.

PROSPERO
Why, that's my dainty Ariel. I shall miss   105
Thee, but yet thou shalt have freedom. So, so, so.
To the King's ship, invisible as thou art.
There shalt thou find the mariners asleep
Under the hatches. The master and the boatswain
Being awake, enforce them to this place,   110
And presently, I prithee.

112. **drink the air:** The phrase "to devour the way" meant to cover ground quickly. Ariel will instead "cover air" quickly.

113. **Or ere:** before

115. **Inhabits:** dwells

116. **fearful:** terrifying

119. **For:** i.e., to provide you with

123. **Whe'er . . . no:** i.e., whether you are he or not

124. **some enchanted trifle:** i.e., an insubstantial magic show; **abuse:** deceive, delude

125. **As late I have been:** i.e., **as I have** lately **been** (deceived, deluded)

129. **An if this be:** i.e., if this exists; **story:** i.e., explanation, narrative

130. **resign:** relinquish, hand over (to you)

131. **wrongs:** wrongdoings

135. **thine age:** i.e., you (who are an old man)

140. **subtleties:** devices, artifices (The word also meant "confections, desserts," a meaning suggested by Prospero's use of the word **taste.**)

142. **brace:** pair

ARIEL
  I drink the air before me, and return
  Or ere your pulse twice beat.   *He exits.*
GONZALO
  All torment, trouble, wonder, and amazement
  Inhabits here. Some heavenly power guide us   115
  Out of this fearful country!
PROSPERO, ⌜*to Alonso*⌝   Behold, sir king,
  The wrongèd Duke of Milan, Prospero.
  For more assurance that a living prince
  Does now speak to thee, I embrace thy body,   120
                    ⌜*He embraces Alonso.*⌝
  And to thee and thy company I bid
  A hearty welcome.
ALONSO   Whe'er thou be'st he or no,
  Or some enchanted trifle to abuse me
  (As late I have been) I not know. Thy pulse   125
  Beats as of flesh and blood; and since I saw thee,
  Th' affliction of my mind amends, with which
  I fear a madness held me. This must crave,
  An if this be at all, a most strange story.
  Thy dukedom I resign, and do entreat   130
  Thou pardon me my wrongs. But how should
    Prospero
  Be living and be here?
PROSPERO, ⌜*to Gonzalo*⌝   First, noble friend,
  Let me embrace thine age, whose honor cannot   135
  Be measured or confined.
GONZALO   Whether this be
  Or be not, I'll not swear.
PROSPERO   You do yet taste
  Some subtleties o' th' isle, that will ⌜not⌝ let you   140
  Believe things certain. Welcome, my friends all.
  ⌜*Aside to Sebastian and Antonio.*⌝ But you, my brace
    of lords, were I so minded,

145. **justify you:** prove you to be

152. **rankest:** greatest; most offensive; **require:** demand

153. **perforce:** by necessity

157. **whom:** i.e., who; **since:** ago

161. **woe:** i.e., woeful, distressed

162. **patience:** i.e., the calm endurance of loss or pain

165. **soft:** gentle, merciful, compassionate

166. **the like loss:** i.e., a **loss like** the one you just described

169. **As great to me as late:** i.e., **as great** a loss **to me,** and as recent

170. **dear:** grievous, dire

176. **mudded:** i.e., buried in the mud

"Graves . . . have waked their sleepers." (5.1.57–58)
From *A Series of Antient . . . Paintings . . . on the Walls of the Chapel . . . at Stratford upon Avon* (etched and published in 1807 by Thomas Fisher).

I here could pluck his Highness' frown upon you
And justify you traitors. At this time 145
I will tell no tales.
SEBASTIAN, ⌜*aside*⌝ The devil speaks in him.
PROSPERO, ⌜*aside to Sebastian*⌝ No.
⌜*To Antonio.*⌝ For you, most wicked sir, whom to
    call brother 150
Would even infect my mouth, I do forgive
Thy rankest fault, all of them, and require
My dukedom of thee, which perforce I know
Thou must restore.
ALONSO   If thou be'st Prospero, 155
Give us particulars of thy preservation,
How thou hast met us here, whom three hours since
Were wracked upon this shore, where I have lost—
How sharp the point of this remembrance is!—
My dear son Ferdinand. 160
PROSPERO   I am woe for 't, sir.
ALONSO
Irreparable is the loss, and patience
Says it is past her cure.
PROSPERO   I rather think
You have not sought her help, of whose soft grace, 165
For the like loss, I have her sovereign aid
And rest myself content.
ALONSO   You the like loss?
PROSPERO
As great to me as late, and supportable
To make the dear loss have I means much weaker 170
Than you may call to comfort you, for I
Have lost my daughter.
ALONSO   A daughter?
O heavens, that they were living both in Naples,
The King and Queen there! That they were, I wish 175
Myself were mudded in that oozy bed

180. **admire:** marvel

182. **do offices of truth:** i.e., perform their truth-telling duties; or, perform their duties truthfully

184. **justled:** jostled, shoved away

186. **of:** from

191. **chronicle:** narrative (with the word's primary meaning of "a detailed historical record" also suggested)

192. **relation:** report

193. **Befitting:** appropriate for

195. **subjects none abroad:** i.e., no **subjects** outside (of my "court")

197. **requite:** repay, reward

199 SD. **discovers:** reveals (probably by pulling a curtain aside)

200. **play me false:** i.e., are cheating

203–4. **for a score ... play:** i.e., you would do so for twenty **kingdoms**—i.e., for less than **the world**—but (because I love you) I would say that you were playing by the rules **wrangle:** contend (but here with the implication of contending unfairly)

206. **A vision of the island:** i.e., the kind of illusory spectacle this **island** produces

Where my son lies!—When did you lose your
   daughter?

PROSPERO
In this last tempest. I perceive these lords
At this encounter do so much admire   180
That they devour their reason, and scarce think
Their eyes do offices of truth, their words
Are natural breath.—But howsoe'er you have
Been justled from your senses, know for certain
That I am Prospero and that very duke   185
Which was thrust forth of Milan, who most
   strangely
Upon this shore, where you were wracked, was
   landed
To be the lord on 't. No more yet of this,   190
For 'tis a chronicle of day by day,
Not a relation for a breakfast, nor
Befitting this first meeting. ⌜*To Alonso.*⌝ Welcome, sir.
This cell's my court. Here have I few attendants,
And subjects none abroad. Pray you, look in.   195
My dukedom since you have given me again,
I will requite you with as good a thing,
At least bring forth a wonder to content you
As much as me my dukedom.
      Here Prospero discovers Ferdinand and Miranda,
                      playing at chess.

MIRANDA, ⌜*to Ferdinand*⌝
Sweet lord, you play me false.   200
FERDINAND   No, my dearest love,
I would not for the world.
MIRANDA
Yes, for a score of kingdoms you should wrangle,
And I would call it fair play.
ALONSO   If this prove   205
A vision of the island, one dear son
Shall I twice lose.

213. **compass thee about:** i.e., encompass you
216. **goodly:** handsome, admirable
217. **brave:** splendid, wonderful
221. **eld'st:** oldest, most lengthy
229. **renown:** report or rumor of his fame
230. **of whom:** i.e., from whom
238. **heaviness:** sorrow
239. **inly:** inwardly

A magician in a magic circle. (5.1.41 SD)
From Christopher Marlowe, *The tragicall historie of . . . Doctor Faustus . . .* (1631).

SEBASTIAN A most high miracle!

FERDINAND, ⌈*seeing Alonso and coming forward*⌉
  Though the seas threaten, they are merciful.
  I have cursed them without cause. ⌈*He kneels.*⌉ 210

ALONSO Now, all the
    blessings
  Of a glad father compass thee about!
  Arise, and say how thou cam'st here.
                  ⌈*Ferdinand stands.*⌉

MIRANDA, ⌈*rising and coming forward*⌉ O wonder! 215
  How many goodly creatures are there here!
  How beauteous mankind is! O, brave new world
  That has such people in 't!

PROSPERO 'Tis new to thee.

ALONSO, ⌈*to Ferdinand*⌉
  What is this maid with whom thou wast at play? 220
  Your eld'st acquaintance cannot be three hours.
  Is she the goddess that hath severed us
  And brought us thus together?

FERDINAND Sir, she is mortal,
  But by immortal providence she's mine. 225
  I chose her when I could not ask my father
  For his advice, nor thought I had one. She
  Is daughter to this famous Duke of Milan,
  Of whom so often I have heard renown,
  But never saw before, of whom I have 230
  Received a second life; and second father
  This lady makes him to me.

ALONSO I am hers.
  But, O, how oddly will it sound that I
  Must ask my child forgiveness! 235

PROSPERO There, sir, stop.
  Let us not burden our remembrances with
  A heaviness that's gone.

GONZALO I have inly wept

243. **chalked forth:** traced out, marked out (as if with chalk)

246. **issue:** offspring

254. **his own:** i.e., himself

257. **still:** always; **his heart:** i.e., the **heart** of anyone

259 SD. **amazedly:** as in a trance, in a state of bewilderment

262. **blasphemy:** i.e., blasphemer

268. **glasses:** i.e., hours (literally, hourglasses); **gave out:** reported

269. **yare:** seaworthy; **bravely:** splendidly

The phoenix. (3.3.28)
Conrad Lycosthenes, *Prodigiorum . . .* (1557).

Or should have spoke ere this. Look down, you 240
  gods,
And on this couple drop a blessèd crown,
For it is you that have chalked forth the way
Which brought us hither.

ALONSO   I say "Amen," Gonzalo. 245

GONZALO
Was Milan thrust from Milan, that his issue
Should become kings of Naples? O, rejoice
Beyond a common joy, and set it down
With gold on lasting pillars: in one voyage
Did Claribel her husband find at Tunis, 250
And Ferdinand, her brother, found a wife
Where he himself was lost; Prospero his dukedom
In a poor isle; and all of us ourselves
When no man was his own.

ALONSO, ⌜*to Ferdinand and Miranda*⌝   Give me your 255
  hands.
Let grief and sorrow still embrace his heart
That doth not wish you joy!

GONZALO   Be it so. Amen.

    Enter Ariel, with the Master and Boatswain
         amazedly following.

O, look, sir, look, sir, here is more of us. 260
I prophesied if a gallows were on land,
This fellow could not drown. Now, blasphemy,
That swear'st grace o'erboard, not an oath on
  shore?
Hast thou no mouth by land? What is the news? 265

BOATSWAIN
The best news is that we have safely found
Our king and company. The next: our ship,
Which, but three glasses since, we gave out split,
Is tight and yare and bravely rigged as when
We first put out to sea. 270

273. **tricksy:** crafty, cunning

274. **strengthen:** increase, grow in strength

278. **of sleep:** i.e., asleep

279–80. **clapped under hatches:** i.e., stowed below deck

281. **several:** diverse

286. **in all her trim:** fully rigged and ready to sail

288. **Cap'ring:** i.e., dancing about joyfully; **On a trice:** in an instant

290. **moping:** in a daze

292. **Bravely:** splendidly

293. **maze:** See note to 3.3.2.

295. **conduct:** director

296. **rectify:** set right

298. **infest:** trouble; **beating on:** hammering at

299. **picked leisure:** i.e., a chosen moment of **leisure**

300–302. **single . . . accidents:** i.e., I alone will explain and make plausible everything that has happened (a response to Alonso's "Some oracle must rectify our knowledge")

ARIEL, ⌈*aside to Prospero*⌉ Sir, all this service
 Have I done since I went.
PROSPERO, ⌈*aside to Ariel*⌉ My tricksy spirit!
ALONSO
 These are not natural events. They strengthen
 From strange to stranger.—Say, how came you 275
  hither?
BOATSWAIN
 If I did think, sir, I were well awake,
 I'd strive to tell you. We were dead of sleep
 And—how, we know not—all clapped under
  hatches, 280
 Where, but even now, with strange and several
  noises
 Of roaring, shrieking, howling, jingling chains,
 And more diversity of sounds, all horrible,
 We were awaked, straightway at liberty, 285
 Where we, in all ⌈her⌉ trim, freshly beheld
 Our royal, good, and gallant ship, our master
 Cap'ring to eye her. On a trice, so please you,
 Even in a dream were we divided from them
 And were brought moping hither. 290
ARIEL, ⌈*aside to Prospero*⌉ Was 't well done?
PROSPERO, ⌈*aside to Ariel*⌉
 Bravely, my diligence. Thou shalt be free.
ALONSO
 This is as strange a maze as e'er men trod,
 And there is in this business more than nature
 Was ever conduct of. Some oracle 295
 Must rectify our knowledge.
PROSPERO   Sir, my liege,
 Do not infest your mind with beating on
 The strangeness of this business. At picked leisure,
 Which shall be shortly, single I'll resolve you, 300
 Which to you shall seem probable, of every
 These happened accidents; till when, be cheerful

306–7. **my gracious sir:** i.e., Alonso

309. **Some few odd:** i.e., a **few**

310–11. **Every man . . . himself:** Stephano (no doubt inadvertently) twists "let every man shift for himself" into an expression of altruism.

312. **Coraggio:** i.e., courage; **bully monster:** i.e., my fine **monster**

313–14. **If . . . head:** i.e., if I can believe my eyes

315. **brave:** splendid

320. **like:** i.e., likely

322. **Mark:** observe, take note of; **badges:** identifying devices worn by servants to indicate whom they serve

323. **true:** accurate, correct; **knave:** villain; servant

325. **That could:** i.e., **that** she **could; make flows and ebbs:** i.e., **make** the sea ebb and flow

326. **her command:** i.e., the moon's sway; **without her power:** i.e., beyond the **power** possessed by **the moon** [line 325]

330. **own:** acknowledge as yours

332. **pinched:** tortured

And think of each thing well. ⌈*Aside to Ariel.*⌉
  Come hither, spirit;
Set Caliban and his companions free.   305
Untie the spell. ⌈*Ariel exits.*⌉ How fares my gracious
  sir?
There are yet missing of your company
Some few odd lads that you remember not.

Enter Ariel, driving in Caliban, Stephano, and Trinculo
in their stolen apparel.

STEPHANO Every man shift for all the rest, and let no 310
  man take care for himself, for all is but fortune.
  Coraggio, bully monster, coraggio.
TRINCULO If these be true spies which I wear in my
  head, here's a goodly sight.
CALIBAN O Setebos, these be brave spirits indeed! How 315
  fine my master is! I am afraid he will chastise me.
SEBASTIAN Ha, ha!
  What things are these, my Lord Antonio?
  Will money buy 'em?
ANTONIO   Very like. One of them 320
  Is a plain fish and no doubt marketable.
PROSPERO
  Mark but the badges of these men, my lords,
  Then say if they be true. This misshapen knave,
  His mother was a witch, and one so strong
  That could control the moon, make flows and ebbs, 325
  And deal in her command without her power.
  These three have robbed me, and this demi-devil,
  For he's a bastard one, had plotted with them
  To take my life. Two of these fellows you
  Must know and own. This thing of darkness I 330
  Acknowledge mine.
CALIBAN   I shall be pinched to death.
ALONSO
  Is not this Stephano, my drunken butler?

335. **reeling ripe:** i.e., drunk enough to reel

336. **gilded 'em:** i.e., flushed their faces

337–40. **How . . . flyblowing:** Three meanings of **pickle** are played on in these lines. "To be **in a pickle**" (i.e., in trouble) is proverbial; "to be pickled" means to be drunk; it also means to be preserved. (If Trinculo's flesh is preserved, it will not decay and attract blowflies.)

344. **sirrah:** a term of address to a male social inferior

349. **look:** i.e., want, expect

350. **trim it:** prepare the cell

352. **grace:** pardon; favor

355. **Go to:** an expression of impatience

356. **luggage:** i.e., the trash you are lugging about

360. **waste:** spend

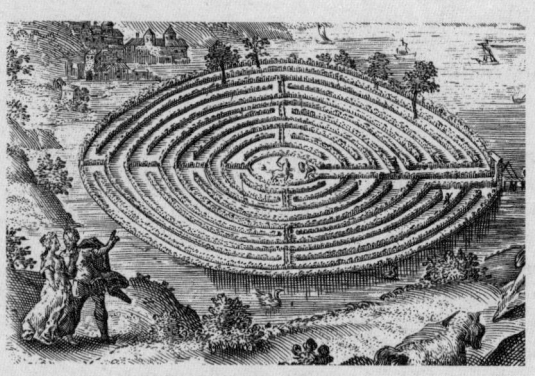

A maze. (3.3.2; 5.1.293)
From *Stirpium, insignium nobilitatis . . .* (1602?).

SEBASTIAN   He is drunk now. Where had he wine?
ALONSO
  And Trinculo is reeling ripe. Where should they   335
  Find this grand liquor that hath gilded 'em?
  ⌜*To Trinculo.*⌝ How cam'st thou in this pickle?
TRINCULO   I have been in such a pickle since I saw you
    last that I fear me will never out of my bones. I
    shall not fear flyblowing.   340
SEBASTIAN   Why, how now, Stephano?
STEPHANO   O, touch me not! I am not Stephano, but a
    cramp.
PROSPERO   You'd be king o' the isle, sirrah?
STEPHANO   I should have been a sore one, then.   345
ALONSO, ⌜*indicating Caliban*⌝
  This is ⌜as⌝ strange ⌜a⌝ thing as e'er I looked on.
PROSPERO
  He is as disproportioned in his manners
  As in his shape. ⌜*To Caliban.*⌝ Go, sirrah, to my cell.
  Take with you your companions. As you look
  To have my pardon, trim it handsomely.   350
CALIBAN
  Ay, that I will, and I'll be wise hereafter
  And seek for grace. What a thrice-double ass
  Was I to take this drunkard for a god,
  And worship this dull fool!
PROSPERO   Go to, away!   355
ALONSO, ⌜*to Stephano and Trinculo*⌝
  Hence, and bestow your luggage where you found it.
SEBASTIAN   Or stole it, rather.
               ⌜*Caliban, Stephano, and Trinculo exit.*⌝
PROSPERO
  Sir, I invite your Highness and your train
  To my poor cell, where you shall take your rest
  For this one night, which part of it I'll waste   360
  With such discourse as, I not doubt, shall make it
  Go quick away: the story of my life

363. **accidents:** events

367. **solemnized:** celebrated with proper ceremony and in due form

368. **retire me:** withdraw, travel

369. **be my grave:** i.e., be about my own mortality

372. **Take:** i.e., **take** possession of, enchant

373. **deliver all:** tell all of it

375. **sail:** i.e., voyage

375–76. **that shall . . . far off:** i.e., **that** you will be able to overtake **your** far-off **royal fleet** (See 1.2.275–80.)

379. **draw near:** These words may invite the other characters into Prospero's cell. (See longer note, page 177.)

Epilogue

---

1. **charms:** magic spells

4. **you:** i.e., the audience

8. **by your spell:** Prospero here turns over to the audience the power of casting spells.

9. **bands:** bonds

10. **help . . . hands:** i.e., through your applause

11. **breath:** from the applause or from their cheers

13. **want:** lack

And the particular accidents gone by
Since I came to this isle. And in the morn
I'll bring you to your ship, and so to Naples,   365
Where I have hope to see the nuptial
Of these our dear-belovèd solemnized,
And thence retire me to my Milan, where
Every third thought shall be my grave.
ALONSO   I long   370
To hear the story of your life, which must
Take the ear strangely.
PROSPERO   I'll deliver all,
And promise you calm seas, auspicious gales,
And sail so expeditious that shall catch   375
Your royal fleet far off. ⌜*Aside to Ariel.*⌝ My Ariel,
    chick,
That is thy charge. Then to the elements
Be free, and fare thou well.—Please you, draw near.
                                              They all exit.

EPILOGUE,

spoken by Prospero.

Now my charms are all o'erthrown,
And what strength I have 's mine own,
Which is most faint. Now 'tis true
I must be here confined by you,
Or sent to Naples. Let me not,   5
Since I have my dukedom got
And pardoned the deceiver, dwell
In this bare island by your spell,
But release me from my bands
With the help of your good hands.   10
Gentle breath of yours my sails
Must fill, or else my project fails,
Which was to please. Now I want
Spirits to enforce, art to enchant,

18. **Mercy itself:** i.e., God in his **mercy; frees:** wins (one) freedom from

19. **crimes:** sins

20. **indulgence:** favor (with wordplay on the theological meaning, where an indulgence frees one from the punishment that would ordinarily be due a sin)

Hymen with his "lamp." (4.1.24, 108)
From Vincenzo Cartari, *Imagines deorum* . . . (1581).

And my ending is despair,   15
Unless I be relieved by prayer,
Which pierces so that it assaults
Mercy itself, and frees all faults.
   As you from crimes would pardoned be,
   Let your indulgence set me free.   20

He exits.

Longer Notes

1.2.293. **Before the time be out:** Here, and in Ariel's speech that follows, the language is that of a master with an indentured servant or an apprentice. Ariel and Prospero speak as though a contract had been signed committing Ariel to serve Prospero faithfully for a certain number of years before Ariel will be given his freedom. It is interesting to note that street magicians in Shakespeare's day had young apprentices who helped them with their conjuring tricks. (See Mowat, "Prospero, Agrippa, and Hocus Pocus," in Further Reading, below.)

1.2.392. **pinched:** The word *pinch* had a much larger set of meanings than we now give it. Victims tortured on the rack, for example, were said to be **pinched;** a pinch could be almost any extremely painful physical sensation or could be the pain caused by the grip of death, of shame, or of remorse. Here it may have its more ordinary sense, but later in the play it often carries these harsher meanings.

1.2.410. **In this hard rock:** In several of Shakespeare's late plays, **rock** often seems to mean "cliff" or some other large mass of stones in which one might find a cave. In Virgil's *Aeneid*, which is echoed frequently in *The Tempest*, the shipwrecked sailors find harbor "under the brow of the fronting cliff [in] a cave of hanging rocks."

1.2.505–9. **Most sure . . . bear me here:** The lines in *Aeneid* 1.327–33 read, in the Loeb translation: "by what name should I call thee, O maiden? for thy face is not mortal . . . ; O goddess surely! . . . Inform us, pray, beneath what sky, on what coasts of the world, we are cast; knowing naught of country or of people, we wander hither driven by wind and huge billows."

1.2.552. ill: According to Neoplatonic philosophy, a beautiful face and body reflect the beauty of the person within. In lines 553–54, Miranda argues that the **temple** of Ferdinand's body is **so fair a house** that even if it were the home of **the ill spirit** (i.e., the devil), good things would try to live there (thus, perhaps, casting out the evil).

2.1.79. widow Dido: Dido was known in two differing sets of narratives. In one set, she was a faithful widow who ruled her country well and died a martyr to her husband's memory; in the other (made famous by Virgil in the *Aeneid*), she became the lover of Aeneas and committed suicide when he left her. This confusion about Dido's story and about the relationship between the ancient Carthage and the more recent Tunis (which some thought was built where Carthage once stood) lies behind the story told by Adrian and Gonzalo and the quibbling of Sebastian and Antonio in lines 77–106.

2.1.162–71, 175–80. I' th' commonwealth . . . people: These passages are based on Montaigne's essay "Of the Cannibals" as translated by John Florio (printed in 1603).

2.2.29. painted: The allusion here and in the following lines seems to be to England's fascination with Native Americans—"Indians"—brought from the New World in the sixteenth century and put on exhibition. The context of this fascination is explored in *"The Tempest:* A Modern Perspective," below.

2.2.58–59. Do you . . . Ind: Stephano speaks here as the knowledgeable European who has read about the strange sights and monsters reported by travelers returned from "the New World." For the phrase **men of Ind,** see Jeremiah 13.23: "May a man **of Ind** change his skin, and the cat of the mountain her spots?" (Bishops' Bible).

3.2.70. pied ninny, patch: While the words **patch** and **pied ninny** are taken as references to Trinculo's profession, there are no other references in the play to his being a Fool, except for the "Names of the Actors" list printed at the end of the Folio text, where Trinculo is called a jester. The origin of this list, however, is unknown. (See "An Introduction to This Text" and the illustration on page 2.)

3.3.64–65. Each . . . warrant of: Because travel was so hazardous, a traveler could deposit a sum with a broker who would agree to pay the traveler five times that sum ("five for one") if the traveler could successfully reach the appointed destination and return.

3.3.69 SD. like a Harpy: This incident is modeled on appearances of harpies to such travelers as Jason, in the *Argonautica*, and Aeneas, in the *Aeneid*. In these stories, the harpies destroy or devour the food of the starving travelers and utter dire prophecies about the travelers' futures. (See "*The Tempest:* A Modern Perspective," below.)

3.3.124–25. But . . . o'er: Sebastian apparently believes that the apparitions he has just encountered are devils. **Legion** is the name of the "unclean spirit" possessing the demoniac in Mark 5.9, whose response to Jesus' question "What is thy name?" was "My name is Legion; for we are many."

4.1.66 SD. Enter Iris: This masque, which begins with Iris's entrance, is modeled on the court masques presented for King James; it includes singing and dancing; it centers on mythological goddesses—Ceres, Juno, and an offstage Venus; it is introduced by **Iris,** the rainbow, messenger of the gods and goddesses. The language of this masque is set apart from the language of the play itself by contorted word order and archaic, markedly "poetic" diction. Some editors have believed that this masque was added to *The Tempest* for the play's performance during the wedding festivities for King James's daughter Elizabeth in 1613.

4.1.97–98. they did plot . . . got: In the story of Ceres and her daughter Persephone, as told by Ovid in Book 5 of the *Metamorphoses*, Venus instructs Cupid to inflame Dis (or Pluto) with love, so that Venus's dominion might extend to the underworld and so that Ceres' daughter might not be allowed to flout Venus by remaining "all her life a Maid unwedded still" (Golding trans., 1567). After Cupid's arrow strikes him, Dis is overcome with desire for Persephone, and he carries her off to the underworld to be his bride.

4.1.138. wise: The late Jeanne Addison Roberts argued that this word should instead be *wife*, and it was thus printed in many editions for several decades. She had found some copies of the 1623 Folio in which, in place of the long *s*, there was an *f*. She argued that during the printing of *The Tempest* for the First Folio, the *f* in *wife* became damaged (i.e., its crossbar was broken), so that in many copies of the Folio the *f* looks like the old long *s*, and the word appears to be *wise*. (See Roberts, "'Wife' and 'Wise'—*The Tempest* 1. 1786," *Studies in Bibliography* 31 [1978]: 203–208.) Inspection of the type in question under great magnification suggests, however, that it is a long *s*, and not an *f;* it appears to be an *f* in some copies because debris has become inked and has printed in such a way as to make the *s* appear an *f*. (See Peter W. M. Blayney's introduction to the 2nd edition of Charlton Hinman's *Norton Facsimile* [1996], p. xxxi [see Further Reading, below].)

5.1.35. **The rarer action:** Montaigne's essay "Of Cruelty" (in Florio's 1603 translation, with spelling modernized) reads: "He that through . . . genuine mildness should . . . contemn injuries received should no doubt perform a rare action. . . . But he who, being touched and stung to the quick with any wrong or offence received, should arm himself with reason against this furiously-blind desire of revenge, and in the end, after a great conflict, yield himself master over it, should doubtless do much more. . . . [T]he one action might be termed goodness, the other virtue."

5.1.42–59. **You elves . . . potent art:** This invocation of spirits draws heavily on Medea's invocation in Book 7 of Ovid's *Metamorphoses*. Shakespeare seems to have used both the original Latin and Golding's 1567 English version.

5.1.50 **Weak masters:** These **elves** and **demi-puppets** seem weak indeed, far removed (in power) from the major supernatural events they have aided Prospero in performing. In Ovid, such elves help Medea only with her control over streams; she uses larger charms for such feats as causing eclipses.

5.1.379. **draw near:** In some productions, the actor playing Prospero, instead of exiting with the other characters, addresses these words to the audience as he moves forward toward the edge of the stage.

Textual Notes

The reading of the present text appears to the left of the square bracket. Unless otherwise noted, the reading to the left of the bracket is from **F,** the First Folio text (upon which this edition is based). The earliest sources of readings not in F are indicated as follows: **F2** is the Second Folio of 1632; **F3** is the Third Folio of 1663–64; **F4** is the Fourth Folio of 1685; **Ed.** is an earlier editor of Shakespeare, beginning with Rowe in 1709. No sources are given for emendations of punctuation or for corrections of obvious typographical errors, like turned letters that produce no known word. **SD** means stage direction; **SP** means speech prefix; **uncorr.** means the first or uncorrected state of the First Folio; **corr.** means the second or corrected state of the First Folio; ~ stands in place of a word already quoted before the square bracket; ∧ indicates the omission of a punctuation mark.

Names of the Actors printed at the end of the play in F

1.1	12.	boatswain] F (Boson)
	22.	councillor] F (Counsellor)
	36.	wi' th'] F (with) *See line 66.*
	36–37.	*A cry within.*) A plague∧] A plague—*A cry within.* F
	38.	SD *2 lines earlier directly after "A cry within." in* F
	50–51.	courses. Off] ~∧ ~ F
	52.	SP MARINERS] F (*Mari.*)
	62.	SD *within:*] ~. F
	66.	wi' th'] F (with')
	70.	furze] F (firrs)
1.2	3.	pour] F (powre)

73. princess∧] ~; F
95. studies.] ~, F
111. that which,] ~, ~∧ F
130. Milan] F *corr.* (*Millaine*); *Millanie* F *uncorr.*
131. royalties] roalties F
133. wi' th'] F (with)
190. divine.] ~, F
207. princes] F (Princesse)
236. bowsprit] F (Bore-spritt)
249–50. vessel, . . . me.] ~; . . . ~∧ F
296. made no] Ed.; made thee no F
318, 337. human] F (humane)
335. she] Ed.; he F
363. Awake] *Pro.* Awake F
391. forth at] Ed.; for that F
415. humane] F
451SD–452, 473SD–474. *Song.* | ARIEL] *Ariel Song.* F
459. SD Burden dispersedly] *2 words earlier in* F
462. *Hark*] *Ar. Hark* F
467. o' th' island.] 'oth'Iland, F
468. wrack,] ~. F
488. is 't?]~ ~∧ F
518. wert] wer't F
556. Speak] *Pros.* Speake F
590. again∧] ~. F

2.1   18–19. entertained∧ . . . offered,] ~, . . . ~∧ F
38. SP ANTONIO] Ed.; *Seb.* F
39. SP SEBASTIAN] Ed.; *Ant.* F
66. gloss] Ed.; glosses F
98. Ay] F (I)
125. kept,] ~. F
133. lose] F (loose)
179. its] F (it)

225. consent.] ~∧ F
261. throes] F (throwes)
311. brother] Brothet F

2.2 17. SD *3 lines earlier in* F
154. o' th'] 'oth F

3.1 2. sets] Ed.; set F
16. busiest] Ed.; busie lest, F
42–43. you, | Chiefly] ~∧ | ~, F
57. peerless] peetlesse F
73. would,] ~∧ F

3.2 3. 'em] em' F
16. light.—] ~∧ F
28. debauched] debosh'd F
59. isle;] ~∧ F
165–66. Wilt come? | TRINCULO] Ed.; *Trin.* Wilt come? F

3.3 22. SD *1 line earlier in* F, *immediately followed by "Enter several . . ."*
24. SD *3 lines earlier in* F
36. islanders] F2; Islands F
40. human] F (humaine)
43. present∧] ~; F
50. SD *26 lines earlier in* F, *immediately following 24 SD, "... salutations," as "and inuiting the King, &c. to eate, they depart."*
55. Will 't] F (Wilt)
83. plume] Ed.; plumbe F
120. bass] F (base)
121. Therefor] F (Therefore)

4.1 9. of her] Ed.; her of F
14. gift] Ed.; guest F
18. rite] F (right)
27. love∧ . . . now,] ~, . . . ~∧ F
57. rein] F (raigne)
58. abstemious] F (abstenious)

68. vetches] F (Fetches)
70. thatched] F (thetchd)
76. poll-clipped] F (pole-clipt)
82. Her] Ed.; here F
113. SD *32 lines earlier in* F
119. *marriage-blessing*] ~, ~ F
126. *with*] *wtth* F
139. SD *3 1/2 lines later in* F
150. sicklemen,] ~∧ F
152. holiday] F (holly day)
158. SD *4 lines earlier in* F, *following ". . . and
      speaks," as "after which to a
      strange . . ."; the spirits*] This ed.;
      they F
177. infirmity.] ~, F
179. repose. . . . two∧] ~, . . . ~, F
181. SD *They exit.*] Ed.; *Exit.* F
181. SD *Enter Ariel.*] *1 line later in* F
200. gorse] F (gosse)
203. filthy-mantled] ~∧ ~ F
213. Humanely] F
216. SD *1 line later in* F
217. them on] Ed.; on them F
235. that,] ~∧ F
258. Let 't] Ed.; let's F

5.1   26. human] F (humane)
        50. bedimmed] F (bedymn'd)
        55. based] F (bass'd)
        69. boiled] Ed.; boile F
        81. Didst] F (*catch-word*); Did F (*text*)
        85. entertained] F2; entertaine F
        92. lies] F3; ly F
        118. Milan] F *corr.* (*Millaine*); *Maillaine* F
             uncorr.
        123. Whe'er] F (Where)
        125. been] F *corr.* (beene); beenee F *uncorr.*

140. isle] F *corr.* (Isle); Islle F *uncorr.*
140. not] F3; nor F
174. Naples] *Nalpes* F
182. truth,] ~: F
274. events] F *corr.* (euents); euens F *uncorr.*
286. her] Ed.; our F
300. shortly, single] ~∧ ~) F
312. monster, coraggio] Monster ∧ *Corasio* F
341. Why] F *corr.*; Who F *uncorr.*
346. as strange a] Ed.; a strange F
372. strangely] starngely F

Epilogue 2. own,] ~. F
20. SD *He exits.*] Exit. | The Scene, an vn-inhabited Island | *Names of the Actors.* [*See page 2.*] FINIS. F

The Tempest:
A Modern Perspective

Barbara A. Mowat

Somewhat past the midpoint of *The Tempest*, King Alonso and his courtiers reach a temporary still point in their journey on Prospero's island. Shipwrecked, they have searched for the lost Prince Ferdinand; now, exhausted, they give up the search. Into this moment of fatigue—and, for Alonso, despair—at the center of what Gonzalo calls their "maze," enters the maze's monster: a Harpy who threatens them with lingering torment worse than any death. For Alonso, the Harpy's recounting of his long-ago crimes against Prospero is "monstrous"; maddened, he rushes off to leap (he thinks) into the sea, to join (he thinks) his drowned son Ferdinand.

King Alonso's confrontation with the Harpy (3.3.23–133) brings together powerfully *The Tempest*'s intricate set of travel stories and its technique of presenting key dramatic moments as theatrical fantasy. The presentation of dancing islanders, a disappearing banquet, and a descending monster is the first big spectacle since the play's opening tempest. The unexpected appearance of these island "spirits," combined with the power of the Harpy's speech, gives the Harpy confrontation a solidity within the story world that seems designed to rivet audience attention. At the same time, audience response to the scene is inevitably colored by curiosity about the "quaint device" that makes the banquet vanish and by awareness of Prospero looking down on his trapped enemies from "the top," commenting on them in asides, and obtrusively turning the Harpy/king encounter into make-believe, first by telling us that the Harpy is only Ariel reciting a speech and, second, by reminding us, just before Alonso's desperate exit to join Ferdinand in the ocean's ooze, that Ferdinand is, at this moment, courting Miranda.

The double signals here—to the powerful moment within the story and to the deliberate theatricality with which the moment is staged—reflect larger double-nesses in this drama. They reflect, first of all, major differences in the temporal and spatial dimensions of the drama's "story" and its "play." *The Tempest*'s "story" stretches over more than twenty-four years and several sea journeys; it embeds elements of the mythological voyages of Aeneas and of Jason and the Argonauts, of the biblical voyages of St. Paul, and of actual contemporary voyages to the new world of Virginia. The "play" that *The Tempest* actually presents is, in contrast, constricted within a plot-time of a single afternoon and confined to the space imagined for an island.[1] Through this particular doubling, Shakespeare creates in *The Tempest* a form that allows him to bring familiar voyage material to the stage in a (literally) spectacular new way.

The "story" that *The Tempest* tells is one of sea voyages—Sycorax's journey from Algiers, Prospero and Miranda's from Milan to the island in the rotten carcass of a butt, Alonso's from Naples to Tunis across the Mediterranean Sea and thence to the island—and, *on* the island, a set of journeys (Ferdinand's across yellow sands; Caliban, Stephano, and Trinculo's through briers and filthy-mantled pools, and Alonso and his men's through strange mazes) that lead, finally, back to the sea and the ship and to yet another sea voyage. This complex narrative, with its immense span of chronological time, its routes stretching over most of the

Mediterranean, its violent separations and losses and its culmination in royal betrothals and restorations, is the kind of story told in the massive novels, popular in Shakespeare's time, called Greek Romances. *The Tempest*'s story could have filled one or more such romance volumes or could have been presented in a narrative-like drama such as Shakespeare himself had created in *Pericles* and *The Winter's Tale*. Instead, within the brief period of *The Tempest*'s supposed action, the narrative of the twenty-four or more years preceding the shipwreck of King Alonso and his courtiers on the island—worked out by Shakespeare in elaborate detail—is told to us elaborately. The second and third scenes of *The Tempest*—that is, 1.2 and 2.1—contain close to half the lines in the play, and close to half of *those* lines are past-tense narration. Through Prospero, through Ariel, through Caliban, through Gonzalo, through Sebastian, through Antonio, characters in our presence (and our present) tell us their pasts.

If we take the sets of narratives embedded in 1.2 and 2.1 and roll them back to where they belong chronologically, the first story (and the most fantastic) is that of the witch Sycorax, her exile on the island, her "littering" of Caliban there, and her imprisoning of Ariel (1.2.308–47)—twelve years before Prospero is thrust forth from Milan. That thrusting-forth is the subject of the next story (next chronologically, that is): the narrative of Antonio's betrayal of Prospero and of Prospero and Miranda's sea journey and arrival on the island (1.2.66–200). Then comes the story of what happened on the island during the next twelve years, a story in which narratives that tell of Caliban (1.2.396–451), of Ariel (1.2.287–306, 340–47), and of Miranda and Prospero (1.2.205–8) overlap and intersect. Finally comes the story from the most recent past—the story of the Princess Claribel and her "loathness" to the marriage arranged by her father (2.1.131–40), of Claribel's wedding in Tunis (2.1.71–111), of the return journey of Alonso and his courtiers (2.1.112–17), and of the shipwreck as described by Ariel (1.2.232–80).

One of the most powerful features of the form Shakespeare crafted in *The Tempest* is that this detailed, complex narrative, told us in the first part of the play, keeps reappearing within the play's action. The story of the coup d'état that expelled Prospero "twelve year since," for example, is made the model for the Antonio/Sebastian assassination plot ("Thy case, dear friend," says Sebastian to Antonio, "shall be my precedent: as thou got'st Milan, I'll come by Naples" [2.1.332–34]); the same story appears at the center of the Harpy's message (3.3.86–93); and it is told yet again by Prospero when, in the play's final scene, he attempts to forgive Antonio (5.1.80–89). Caliban's story—"this island is mine"; "I serve a tyrant"—is repeated by him again and again. The story of Sycorax, who died years before the dramatic "now," is alluded to so often—her powers described one last time by Prospero even as the play is ending (5.1.323–26)—that she seems to haunt the play, as does the absent, distant, unhappy Claribel.

As the play reaches its conclusion, each of the stories recounted in the early narrative scenes is conjured up a final time, though the pressure now is toward the future—toward the nuptials of the royal couple, toward a royal lineage with Prospero's heirs as kings of Naples. As that virtual future is created, the structuring process of the opening scenes is reversed: where narrative was there incorporated into the play, now the play opens back out into the next pages of the narrative from which it had emerged. As we watch and listen, the play we have been experiencing moves into the past, becomes a moment in the tale Prospero promises to tell to the voyagers—"such discourse as . . . shall make [the night] / Go quick away: the story of my life / And the particular accidents gone by / Since I came to this isle" (5.1.361–64). As Alonso notes, this is a "story . . . which must / Take the ear strangely" (5.1.371–72).

By folding the story into the play and then unfolding the play into its own virtual narrative future, Shakespeare creates a form in which past and future press on the present dramatic moment with peculiar intensity. We sense this throughout the play, but see it with special clarity in the confrontation between Alonso and the Harpy. The Harpy brings the past to Alonso as a burden Alonso must pick up—an intolerable burden for Alonso, who goes mad under the simultaneous recognition of his guilt and its consequences, given to him as Time Past, Time Present, and Time Future. In Time Past: "you . . . / From Milan did supplant good Prospero, / Exposed unto the sea . . . / Him and his innocent child" (3.3.87–90); in Time Present: "for which foul deed, / The powers . . . have / Incensed the seas and shores, yea, all the creatures / Against your peace. Thee of thy son, Alonso, / They have bereft" (90–94); and finally, in Time Future: "Ling'ring perdition . . . shall step by step attend / You and your ways, whose wraths to guard you from— / Which here, in this most desolate isle, else falls / Upon your heads—is nothing but heart's sorrow / And a clear life ensuing" (95–101). This pressure of past and future on the present moment—a pressure that is created in large part by the way Shakespeare folds chronological time into plot-time, and that we feel throughout the play in Prospero's tension, in Ariel's restiveness, in Caliban's fury—makes believable in *The Tempest* that which is normally suspect: namely, instant repentance, instant inner transformation. Because the dramatic present is so permeated with the play's virtual past, so pressured by the future—the six o'clock toward which the play rushes, after which

Time as Opportunity will be gone—Alonso's anguished repentance, his descent into silence, madness, and unceasing tears, his immediate surrender of Milan to Prospero and the reward of being given back his lost son, can all take place in moments, and can, even so, seem credible and wonderful.

The interplay between *The Tempest*'s elaborate voyage story and its tightly constricted "play" is not the only doubleness toward which the drama's Harpy/king encounter points us. It points as well to two kinds of travel tales embedded in the drama: ancient, fictional voyage narratives and contemporary travelers' tales buzzing around London at the time the play was being written. The Harpy/king encounter is shaped as a sequence of verbal and visual events that in effect reenact and thus recall ancient confrontations between harpies and sea voyagers. In each of these harpy incidents—from the third century B.C.E. *Argonautica* through the first century B.C.E. *Aeneid* to *The Tempest* itself—harpies are ministers of the gods sent to punish those who have angered the gods; they punish by devouring or despoiling food; and they are associated with dire prophecies. *The Tempest*'s enactment of the harpy encounter is thus one in a line of harpy stories stretching into the past from this island and this set of voyagers to Aeneas, and through Aeneas back to Jason and the crucial encounter between the terrible harpies (the "hounds of mighty Zeus") and the Argonauts.[2] In replicating the sequence of events of voyagers meeting harpies, combining details from Jason's story and from the *Aeneid*, Shakespeare directs attention to the specific context in which such harpy confrontations appear and within which *The Tempest* clearly belongs— that of literary fictional voyages.

At the same time, he surrounds the encounter with dialogue that would remind his audience of present-day voyages of their own fellow Londoners. Geographical expansion, around-the-world journeys, explorations of the new world of the Americas had heightened the stay-at-homes' fascination with the strange creatures reported by travelers. Real-world creatures like crocodiles and hippopotami, fantastic creatures like unicorns and griffins, reported monstrosities like the men whose heads grow beneath their shoulders—all were, at the time, equally real (or unreal) and equally fascinating. The dialogue preceding the Harpy's descent in *The Tempest* centers on such fabulous creatures. When the supposed "islanders"—creatures of "monstrous shape"—appear, bringing in the banquet, Sebastian says: "Now I will believe / That there are unicorns, that in Arabia / There is one tree, the phoenix' throne, one phoenix / At this hour reigning there." "Travelers ne'er did lie," says Antonio, "Though fools at home condemn 'em." Gonzalo adds, "If in Naples / I should report this now, would they believe me? / If I should say I saw such islanders . . ." (3.3.26–36). It is into this dialogue-context that the Harpy descends—that is, into a discussion of fantastic travelers' tales and fabulous creatures.

When the Harpy—one of these creatures—actually appears, claps its wings upon the table, and somehow makes the food disappear (3.3.69 SD), she is very real to Alonso and his men—as real as the harpies were to Jason and to Aeneas; as real as the hippopotami and anthropophagi were to fifteenth-century explorers; as real as is Caliban, the monster mooncalf, to his discoverers Stephano and Trinculo. The attempts to kill the Harpy are classical responses—that is, they are the responses of Jason and Aeneas when confronted by the terrible bird-women. The response of Stephano and Trinculo to their man-monster is a more typically sixteenth-century response to the fabulous. When, for example, Stephano finds Trinculo and Caliban huddled under a cloak and thinks he has discovered a "most delicate monster" with "four legs and two voices" (2.2.92–93), he responds with the greed that we associate with Martin Frobisher and other sixteenth-century New World explorers who brought natives from North America to England to put on display: "If I can recover him," says Stephano, "and keep him tame and get to Naples with him, he's a present for any emperor that ever trod on neat's leather. . . . He shall pay for him that hath him, and that soundly" (2.2.69–81). Trinculo had responded with equal greed to his first sight of the frightened Caliban:

> What have we here, a man or a fish? . . . A strange fish. Were I in England . . . and had but this fish painted, not a holiday fool there but would give a piece of silver. There would this monster make a man. Any strange beast there makes a man. When they will not give a doit to relieve a lame beggar, they will lay out ten to see a dead Indian.
>
> (2.2.25–34)

While the finding and subjugating of "wild men" was a feature that ancient and New World voyage stories held in common (for example, Jupiter promises that Aeneas, as the climax of his sea journeys, will "wage a great war in Italy, and . . . crush wild peoples and set up laws for men and build walls"[3]), Prospero's subjugation of Caliban has, since the 1980s, been seen as having a particularly New World flavor. The play itself, no matter how steeped it is in ancient voyage literature and no matter how much emphasis it places on its Mediterranean setting, is also a representation of New World exploration. While it retells the stories of Aeneas and of Jason, it also stages a particular Virginia voyage that, in 1610–11, was the topic of sermons, published government accounts, and first-person epistles, many of which Shakespeare drew on in crafting *The Tempest*. The story, in brief, goes as follows: A fleet of ships set out in 1609 from England carrying a new governor—Sir Thomas Gates—to the struggling Virginia colony in Jamestown. The fleet was caught in a tempest off the coast of Bermuda. All of the ships survived the storm and sailed on to Virginia—except the flagship, the *Sea Venture*, carrying the governor, the admiral of the fleet, and other important officials. A year later, the exhausted and dispirited colonists in Jamestown were astounded when two boats sailed up the James River carrying the supposedly drowned governor and his companions. The crew and passengers on the flagship had survived the storm, had lived for a year in the Bermudas, had built new ships, and had made it safely to Virginia. News of the happy ending to this "tragicomedy," as one who reported the story called it, soon reached London, and many details of the story are preserved in *The Tempest*.

Among such details may be the disturbing picture of the relationship of the "Indians" and the "settlers" in Jamestown, represented perhaps in Caliban and his relationship with Prospero. In one of the documents used by Shakespeare in writing *The Tempest*, William Strachey describes an incident in which "certain Indians," finding a man alone, "seized the poor fellow and led him up in to the woods and sacrificed him." Strachey writes that the lieutenant governor was very disturbed by this incident, since hitherto he "would not by any means be wrought to a violent proceeding against them [i.e., the Indians] for all the practices of villainy with which they daily endangered our men." This incident, though, made him "well perceive" that "fair and noble treatment" had little effect "upon a barbarous disposition," and "therefore . . . purposed to be revenged." The revenge took the form of an attack upon an Indian village.[4]

As we read Strachey's account today, we find much in the behavior of the settlers toward the natives that is appalling, so that the account is not for us simply that of "good white men" against "bad Indians," as it was for Strachey. In the same way, whether or not this particular lieutenant governor and these treacherous "Indians" are represented in *The Tempest*, Shakespeare's decision to include a "wild man" among his island's cast of characters, and (as Stephen Greenblatt notes) to place him in opposition to a European prince whose power lies in his language and his books,[5] has, in the past few decades, raised a host of questions about the play. *The Tempest* was written just as England was beginning what would become massive empire-building through the subjugating of others and the possessing of their lands. European nations— Spain, in particular—had already taken over major land areas, and Shakespeare and his contemporaries had available to them many accounts of native peoples and of European colonizers' treatment of such peoples. Many such accounts are like Strachey's: they describe a barbarous people who refuse to be "civilized," who have no language, who have a "nature" on which "nurture will never stick" (as Prospero says of Caliban). Other accounts describe instead cultural differences in which that which is different is not necessarily inferior or "barbarous." When Gonzalo says (at 2.1.157–60), "Had I plantation [i.e., colonization] of this isle . . . And were the king on 't, what would I do?" he answers his own question by describing the Utopia he would set up (lines 162–84), taking his description from Montaigne's essay "Of the Cannibals." In this essay, Montaigne ("whose supple mind," writes Ronald Wright, "exemplifies Western civilization at its best"[6]) argues in effect that American "savages" are in many ways more moral, more humane people than so-called civilized Europeans.

As with so much of *The Tempest*, Caliban may be seen as representing two quite different images. Shakespeare gives him negative traits reminiscent of early modern descriptions of New World natives (traits that now seem to smack of racist responses to the strange and to the Other) while giving him at the same time a richly poetic language and a sensitive awareness of nature and the supernatural. He places Caliban in relation to Prospero (as Caliban's master and the island's "colonizer"), to Miranda (as the girl who taught Caliban language and whom he tried to rape), and indirectly to Ferdinand (who, like Caliban, is made to carry logs and who will father Miranda's children as Caliban had wished to do). Thus, for many critics, Shakespeare creates in the center of this otherworldly play a confrontation that speaks eloquently to readers and audiences living with the aftereffects of the massive colonizing of the eighteenth and nineteenth centuries and observing the continuing life of "empire" in the interactions between the powerful and the formerly colonized states.[7] As many such readers and audiences look back at the centuries of colonization of the Americas, Africa, and India from, as it were, Caliban's perspective, they see *The Tempest*, once considered Shakespeare's most serene, most lyrical play, as his representation, for good or ill, of the colonizing and the colonized.[8]

This relatively new interest in the colonization depicted in *The Tempest* has had a profound impact on attitudes toward Prospero. For centuries seen as spokesman for Shakespeare himself, as the benign magician-artist who presides like a god over an otherworldly kingdom, Prospero is now perceived by many as one of Shakespeare's most complex creations. He

brings to the island books, Old World language, and
the power to hurt and to control; he thus figures an
early form of the colonizer. But he carries with him
other, complicating associations. He is, for example, a
figure familiar in voyage romances popular in Shakespeare's day. He reminds us of the hermit magician (or
exiled doctor, or some equivalent) in Greek Romance
tales who comes to the aid of heroes and heroines,
protects them, heals them, often teaches them who
they really are. In such stories, the focus is always
on the lost, shipwrecked, searching man or woman—
that is, on the Alonso figure or the Ferdinand or the
Miranda figure. In *The Tempest*, Prospero, the hermit
magician, is center stage, and the lost, shipwrecked,
and searching are seen by us through him and in relation to him. Prospero thus carries a kind of power and
an aura of ultimately benevolent intention that com-
plicates the colonizer image.

Prospero is also the creator of the maze in which the
other characters find themselves—"as strange a maze
as e'er men trod," says Alonso (5.1.293)—and thus carries yet other complicating associations. The scene of
the Harpy/king encounter opens with Gonzalo's "Here's
a maze trod indeed through forthrights and meanders," a statement that picks up suggestively Ovid's
description of that most infamous of mazes, created by
Daedalus to enclose the Minotaur. The Daedalus story
has unexpected but rich links with *The Tempest*. Daedalus, the quintessential artist/engineer/magician, built
the maze to sty the monstrous creature that he had
helped to bring into being. (It was sired by a bull on
King Minos's queen, but it was Daedalus who had lured
the bull to the queen, encasing her, at her urgings, in
the wooden shape of a cow.) Having built the maze,
Daedalus (in Golding's 1567 translation of Ovid's *Metamorphoses*) "scarce himselfe could find the meanes to

winde himselfe well out / So busie and so intricate" was the labyrinth he had created (Book 8, lines 211–24).

The story of the maze and its Minotaur is a familiar one, involving the sacrifice of Greek youths to the bloodthirsty Minotaur, an annual horror that stopped only with Theseus's slaughter of the Minotaur and his escape from the maze through the aid of King Minos's daughter, Ariadne, whom Theseus marries and then abandons. Less familiar is the connection between the story of the maze and that of Daedalus and his son Icarus's flight from the island of Crete:

> Now in this while [when Theseus was overcoming
>   the Minotaur] gan Daedalus a wearinesse to take
> Of living like a banisht man and prisoner such a
>   time
> In Crete, and longed in his heart to see his native
>   Clime.
> But Seas enclosed him as if he had in prison be.
> Then thought he: though both Sea and Land King
>   Minos stop fro me,
> I am assurde he cannot stop the Aire and open
>   Skie. . . .
>
> (lines 245–50)

It is at this point that Daedalus turns to "uncoth Arts" (i.e., magic), bending "the force of all his wits / To alter natures course by craft"—and he constructs the famous wings that take him home, at the cost of the life of his son, who falls into the sea and drowns.

When Prospero stands "on the top," looking down and commenting on the trapped figures below him, he to some extent figures the magician/artist Daedalus. Throughout the play he, like Daedalus, is almost trapped in his own intricate maze, an exile who "gan . . . a weariness to take / Of living like a banisht man and prisoner such a time," who "longed in his heart to see his native Clime," and who thus bent "the force of all his wits" and his magic powers to find a way to get himself and his child home. The associations of Prospero with Daedalus, his maze, and his magic flight are less accessible to us today than they would have been to an early-modern audience. But the sense of Prospero's weariness, of his hatred of exile, of the danger facing him as he heads back to Milan having abjured his magic—these complicating emotional factors, even without a specific awareness of the Daedalus parallels, are available to us. We notice them especially in Prospero's epilogue, where he begs our help in wafting him off the island and safely back home.

Like *The Tempest* itself, then, Prospero is complicated, double. He, like the play, is woven from a variety of story materials and, like the play, he represents a particular moment, the moment at which began a period of colonizing and empire building that would completely alter the world, leaving a legacy with which we still live. But he, like the play, also embodies ancient stories of travel and exile and the emotions that accompany them. And *The Tempest*'s nineteenth- and twentieth-century retellings and sequels (Browning's "Caliban on Setebos," Aimé Césaire's *Une Tempête*, Auden's "The Sea and the Mirror," and such film versions as *Forbidden Planet* and Peter Greenaway's *Prospero's Books*, to name but a few) suggest that those stories and emotions have continued to intrigue. The magician fascinates, the journey and the maze still tempt, despite the near certainty that magic—like all power—tends to corrupt and that islands and labyrinths hold as many monsters as they do "revels."

---

1. I am using the word "story" here both in its general sense of a narration of events and in the more particular sense that translates the Russian formalists'

term *fabula*—that is, the events sequenced in chronological order. The formalists contrast the *fabula* with the *szujet*—the fiction as structured by the author (a term I translate as "play"). See Keir Elam's *The Semiotics of Theatre and Drama* (London: Methuen, 1980), pp. 119–26.

2. See Barbara A. Mowat, "'And that's true, too': Structures and Meaning in *The Tempest*," *Renaissance Papers 1976*, pp. 37–50. The pertinent sections of the Argonaut stories are Apollonius Rhodius, *Argonautica* 2.178–535 (quotation, line 289), and Valerius Flaccus, *Argonautica* 4.422–636; Virgil's account of the Harpies as encountered by Aeneas and his men is found in *Aeneid* 3.210–69.

3. *Aeneid* 1.261–64 (Guildford trans.).

4. William Strachey, "A True Reportory of the Wreck and Redemption of Sir Thomas Gates, Knight," in *A Voyage to Virginia in 1609*, ed. Louis B. Wright, pp. 1–101, esp. pp. 88–89. [See Further Reading, below.]

5. Stephen Greenblatt, "Learning to Curse: Aspects of Linguistic Colonialism in the Sixteenth Century," in *Learning to Curse: Essays in Early Modern Culture*, pp. 23–26. [See Further Reading, below.]

6. Ronald Wright, *Stolen Continents: The "New World" Through Indian Eyes* (Toronto: Penguin Books, 1993).

7. See Edward W. Said, "Empire, Geography, and Culture" and "Images of the Past, Pure and Impure," in *Culture and Imperialism* (New York: Alfred A. Knopf, 1993), pp. 3–14, 15–19.

8. For example, in "Nymphs and reapers heavily vanish: the discursive con-texts of *The Tempest*," in *Alternative Shakespeares*, ed. John Drakakis (London: Methuen, 1985 [pp. 191–205]), Francis Barker and Peter Hulme state that "the discourse of colonialism" provides the "dominant discursive contexts" for the play.

Further Reading

The Tempest

Auden, W. H. "The Sea and the Mirror: A Commentary on Shakespeare's *The Tempest*." In *For the Time Being*. New York: Random House, 1944; London: Faber and Faber, 1945. [The poem has been included in all editions of *The Collected Poetry of W. H. Auden* (Random House) since 1945.]

Constructed as a series of dramatic monologues, lyric intermezzi, and one prose monologue, Auden's long poetic reflection on Shakespeare's play—variously labeled a fantasy, a parable, and an allegory—picks up just after the moment the play's action ends. Between the Preface ("The Stage Manager to the Critics") and the Postscript ("Ariel to Caliban. Echo by the Prompter") are three chapters: "Prospero to Ariel," "The Supporting Cast, Sotto Voce," and "Caliban to the Audience." In the first chapter, a seven-stanza monologue, Prospero, as he packs for his return to Milan, talks to Ariel about the very questions left at the end of Shakespeare's play: about Prospero's thoughts on giving up his magic, about Miranda's leaving to marry Ferdinand, about Antonio's refusing reconciliation. The second section is a set of monologues in which each member of "the supporting cast" (Antonio, Ferdinand, Stephano, Gonzalo, Adrian and Francisco, Alonso, Master and Boatswain, Sebastian, Trinculo, and Miranda) is given a poem in which they explain themselves, each followed by a bitter or ironic rejoinder from Antonio. In the final (prose) part, Auden speaks through Caliban in a dense reflection on nature and art. This section concludes with Caliban's exhortation to recognize the blessedness of the secular world of mutability and becoming. "It is just here, among the ruins and the bones, that we may rejoice in the perfected Work which is not ours."

Bigliazzi, Silvia, and Lisanna Calvi, eds. *Revisiting "The Tempest": The Capacity to Signify*. New York: Palgrave Macmillan, 2014.

In an effort to understand *The Tempest*'s "widespread reticence ... ambiguity and contradictions ... as a fertile source of significance," this collection of fourteen new essays focuses on the concept of meaning as it relates to allegory, genre, time-space, spectacle, and the magical realism of film. The individual essays range from "investigations of the play's position within the European early modern dramatic heritage to its 'domestic' rewritings and/or adaptations in diverse theatrical contexts and media, while also interrogating the play's own resistance to interpretation." Andrew Gurr's prologue *"The Tempest* as Theatrical Magic" provides an overview of the play's critical history, specifically as it relates to *The Tempest*'s theatricality and its "conscious, yet controversial, allegorisation of Prospero as the Bard since the early nineteenth century." Serving as an epilogue, Kathleen E. McLuskie's essay "'Abstraction and Allegory': Making *The Tempest* Mean" suggests future perspectives on the "question of meaning-making" in the play. The eleven essays constituting the core of the volume are: Richard Andrews, *"The Tempest* and Italian Improvised Theatre"; Robert Henke, "Pastoral Tragicomedy and *The Tempest*"; Roger Holdsworth, "The Jonsonian *Tempest*"; Alessandro Serpieri, "The Labyrinth and the Oracle"; Silvia Bigliazzi, "'Dost thou hear?' On the Rhetoric of Narrative in *The Tempest*"; Keir Elam, "A Tempestuous Noise: On the Acoustics and Vocalics of Storms"; Lisanna Calvi, "'Suppos'd to be rais'd by Magick', or *The Tempest* 'made fit'"; Lucia Nigri, "'Lost in Visual Pleasure': Charles Kean's Production of *The Tempest*"; Peter Holland, "Magical Realism: Raising Storms and Other Quaint Devices"; Eleonora Oggiano, "'This is a most majestic vision': Performing Prospero's Masque on Screen"; and Alessandra Squeo, "Shakespeare's Hypertextual Performances: Remediating *The Tempest* in Prospero's Books." In an afterword titled "Is there a *Tempest* Problem?" Ewan Fernie dismisses the "'problem' of meaning-making altogether, paradoxically suggesting the possibility for a meaning beyond meaning." Proposing to look at *The Tempest* "as at a mystical play, not in a metaphysical sense, but as both 'invested in the life of the island' and '*directing attention away from itself as drama*,'" Fernie invites us to "transcend . . . Prospero's colonialist identity and identify ourselves with his final renunciation of the desire to know and be in control intellectually and of others." In their intertextual exploration of the play's "signifying potential" for the third millennium, the contributors to *Revisiting "The Tempest"* do not provide new meanings; instead, they examine "how this drama makes meaning and reanimates it through time."

Breight, Curt. "'Treason doth never prosper': *The Tempest* and the Discourse of Treason." *Shakespeare Quarterly* 41 (1990): 1–28.

Breight reads *The Tempest* as "a series of conspiracies, [which] can be inserted into a vast discourse of treason that became an increasingly central response to difficult social problems in late Elizabethan and early Jacobean London." *The Tempest*, however, presents Prospero as stage-managing fictional conspiracies, thereby calling attention subversively to the possibility that so-called treason plots (such as the Gunpowder Plot) put down so bloodily by English monarchs might, like the plots in *The Tempest*, have been stage-managed by the monarchs for the purpose of displaying their power in crushing such "plots." To illustrate the play's "conspiratorial psychology," Breight considers five episodes: "the narrative control and 'freezing' of Ferdinand in 1.2; the frustration of Antonio's and Sebastian's assassination attempt in 2.1; the maddening of the upper-class conspirators in 3.3; the frustration of the lower-class conspirators in 4.1; and the political rehabilitation of Prospero and heir(s) in the final scene." Breight's recontextualization of the play leads him to conclude that Prospero's enemies are ultimately spared "not for sentimental reasons but for reasons of state." Prospero may seem to abandon power through his abjuration of magic, "but the magic has served its purpose," not only restoring him to political control of Milan but also assuring him of dynastic control of both Milan and Naples through Miranda's marriage. "Most importantly," he has kept his former enemies from ever knowing either the extent or the origin of his supernatural power. "What Prospero has learned and the audience is allowed to see [through Shakespeare's 'clever demystification of various official strategies within the discourse of treason'] is the art of politics. Prospero—by means of magical power no longer necessary—has become a politician."

Brevik, Frank W. *"The Tempest" and New World-Utopian Politics*. New York: Palgrave Macmillan, 2012.

Brevik's study of New World and Americanist utopian politics in *The Tempest* examines "paradigm shifts in literary criticism" over the past sixty years that "have all but reinscribed [Shakespeare's text] into a fiercely political palimpsest grounded in historical events like colonialism or even prophetically envisioning postcolonial issues." In the course of tracing and challenging major recent political interpretations of the play, the author "problematize[s] the by now hegemonic views that [it] has a dominant New World dimension, reject[s] the idea that Caliban can be seen as a Native American or African slave [preferring instead to view him as a figure from Old World mythology and folklore], and [seeks to] disprove textually the premise that the play unproblematically addresses a uniquely Western colonial history and post-colonial plight." Following an introduction that addresses the limitations of New Historicist and Cultural Materialist interpretations ("The Rampant Politicization of *Tempest* Criticism and Its Recent Discontents") are seven chapters: (1) "Teaching *The Tempest* in an American-Adamic Context: The New World Orthodoxy as Multicultural Pedagogy," (2) "Such Maps as Dreams Are Made On: Discourse, Utopian Geography, and *The Tempest*'s Island," (3) "Calibans Anonymous: The Journey from Text to Self in Modern Criticism," (4) "*The Tempest* Beyond Post-Colonial Politics: Vargas Llosa's *The Storyteller* as Topical Retrotext," (5) "'Any Strange Beast There Makes a Man': New World Manliness as Old World Kingliness in *The Tempest*," (6) "'Thought Is Free:': *The Tempest*, Freedom of Expression, and the New World," and (7) "Toward a Post-1989 Reading of *The Tempest*." A conclusion titled "Readers vs. Text in the Age of Democracy: The Formalist *Tempest* or Presentist '*Tempests*'?" rounds out the volume. Brevik looks at the characters not as "political creatures . . . [but] as primarily ethical beings, [whose] desires are religious, pastoral, and freedom-seeking in nature," and at the setting not as a "*de facto* New World" but as a "floating island . . . perpetually unstable and literally utopian—that is, *nowhere*." Such a perspective allows him to expand the play's literary and cultural contexts to include Virgilian, European, African, and American from the pioneers to the present day. *The Tempest* "can thus be said to deal with the power to speak and the power to disobey in a way that is both a subversive and an important part of the play's utopian ethos."

Brown, Paul. "'This thing of darkness I acknowledge mine': *The Tempest* and the discourse of colonialism." In *Political Shakespeare: New Essays in Cultural Materialism,* edited by Jonathan Dollimore and Alan Sinfield, pp. 48–71. 2nd ed. Manchester: Manchester University Press, 1994.

Brown's "repunctuation" of *The Tempest* in the context of colonialist discourses about both the New World and Ireland (the latter supplying the "richest and most fraught discussion of colonialism" at the time of the play's inception) "seeks to demonstrate that *The Tempest* is not simply a reflection of colonialist practices but an intervention in an ambivalent and even contradictory discourse" that does not merely "announce a triumph for civility" but must also "continually *produce* it, . . . work [that] involves struggle and risk." Finding the play to be implicated in the process of "'euphemisation,' the effacement of power," Brown argues that while *The Tempest* mystifies power in its magical narrative of sea change, it also exposes the operations of power in Prospero's enslavement and oppression of Caliban, whose "discursive strategies" show him to have "mastered enough of the lessons of civility to ensure that its interpellation of him as simply savage, 'a born devil' (4.1.211), is inadequate": "Ostensibly produced as an other to provide the pretext for the exercise of naked power, he is also a producer, provoking reaction in the master" (see, e.g., Caliban's failure to come when called [1.2.375–84] and his own narrative in which Prospero becomes the "usurping other to Caliban's initial monarchy and hospitality" [395–418]).

Informed by the binaries of civility and incivility, mastery and masterlessness, order and disorder, and the malleable and the irreformable, *The Tempest* "declares no all-embracing triumph for colonialism"; it serves instead "as a limit text in which the characteristic operations of colonialist discourse may be discerned—as an instrument of exploitation, a register of beleaguerment and a site of radical ambivalence."

DiPietro, Cary. "Performing Place in *The Tempest*." In *Shakespeare and the Urgency of Now*, edited by Cary DiPietro and Hugh Grady, pp. 83–102. New York: Palgrave Macmillan, 2013.

Concerned with "where . . . Shakespeare figure[s] in our changing world" and with "how . . . economic, environmental and institutional pressures interpenetrate Shakespeare as a cultural enterprise," DiPietro's presentist approach to *The Tempest* explores the ecological relationship between humans and their surrounding environment. As a portal into the play's "scenic wonders," DiPietro uses the capacity for disembodied travel supplied by such modern sophisticated imaging technologies as Google Maps and Google Earth (1) to focus on how theatrical performance evokes negative and positive connections to place and (2) to consider the implications of such "self-defining attachments" for a better understanding "of ourselves and others [as] shaped by our sense of belonging to particular places in the world." Because of the "apparent placeless-ness" of Prospero's unnamed island—set somewhere in the Mediterranean but filled with allusions to the New World and resonant with Arcadian qualities suggestive of the English pastoral—*The Tempest* "constitutes a promising site for the discussion of the performance of place" and for issues relating to the "unmooring of the modern subject from the premodern attachment to local places." Di Pietro explores how Shakespeare uses clear and vivid ekphrastic rhetoric (see, e.g., 3.2.148–56, 3.3.45–49, and 4.1.137–39), pastoral conventions, and the imagery of colonial discourse to evoke an "aestheticized" sense of place that we are invited to think of as "unreal," as, in the wedding masque, nothing more than "the baseless fabric of [a] vision" (4.1.168): "In a moment that both instantiates and simultaneously challenges the distinction between the virtual and the real, Prospero compares the illusory quality of theatrical artifice to the 'insubstantial pageant' [4.1.172] of our own subjective experience of the world [173–75]. . . . And so, in a self-consciously theatrical gesture, Prospero detaches our existence from our physical surroundings and consciousness is absorbed into a singularity with aesthetic artifice, early modern virtual reality."

Dubrow, Heather. "Delivery Rooms: Towards a Reconsideration of the Conclusion of *The Tempest*." In *Essays in Memory of Richard Helgerson: Laureations*, edited by Roze Hentschell and Kathy Lavezzo, pp. 73–90. Newark, Delaware: University of Delaware Press, 2012.

In a close reading of 5.1, Dubrow attends to "word choice, word meanings, word order, meter," and "emotional deixis" (i.e., the "affective proximity" of words like *this*, *that*, and *here*) to rethink the problem of closure in *The Tempest*. Focusing on the "knottiness" of Prospero's "I'll deliver all" (5.1.373) in the context of key passages leading up to it (5.1.42–66, 145–46, and 370–72), she demonstrates "how the phrase offers a dense and provocative commentary on major themes and problems engaged throughout [the play], namely interrelated issues of power, magic, storytelling and conquest." Her emphasis on the multivalence of "deliver" offers a new perspective on "whether the play and its principal character effect—or merely affect—

reconciliation and renunciation." Dubrow widens the semantic range of "deliver" beyond its usual gloss as "recount" to include distributing, setting free, rescuing, delivering a blow, being delivered to a dreadful fate, handing over a document, and giving birth. The word "deliver," in short, is "anti-closural"; its multiple meanings hold the key to a tension, running throughout the scene, between Prospero's wanting to give up his magical power and his desiring to hold on to it. If we see Prospero as a seductive, coercive teller of tales that "must / Take the ear strangely" (5.1.371–72) and that "may be neither objective nor reliable," there is no reason to accept his promise to "deliver all" as benignly conclusive. On the contrary, the line "raises the possibility that the story Prospero undertakes to relate at the end of the scene may be not a logical stage in the process of renouncing his magic but rather a theatrical stage for enacting and preserving it," i.e., "another power play, not a rejection but a continuation of the way his earlier stories have involved domination." *The Tempest*, then, is a play that resists closure, with Prospero achieving neither reconciliation nor renunciation. In the final pages of the essay, Dubrow calls for a "manifesto on behalf of a depoliticized and pluralist 'New' New Criticism. By showing how materialist and performance criticism have informed her close reading of the play, she demonstrates that such approaches need not be mutually exclusive.

Greenblatt, Stephen J. "Learning to Curse: Aspects of Linguistic Colonialism in the Sixteenth Century." In *Learning to Curse: Essays in Early Modern Culture*, pp. 16–39. New York: Routledge, 1990.

Greenblatt maps out the Renaissance humanist notion that "savages of America were without eloquence or even without language," an opinion that justified the denial to these "savages" of any integrity or identity of their own. In *The Tempest*, "the startling encounter between a lettered and an unlettered culture is heightened, almost parodied, in the relationship between a European whose entire source of power is his library and a savage who had no speech at all before the European's arrival." Some critics have seen Shakespeare the dramatist as the equivalent of a colonist, seeking to impose both the shape of the colonist's own culture and the embodiment of his own speech on the world he discovers; Greenblatt, however, contends that Shakespeare appears ambivalent about this "hold[ing] up the mirror to empire," in that, while the dramatist's depiction of Caliban participates in the colonialist opinion, it goes beyond it to reveal the character as having moments of eloquence. Examples include Caliban's "devastatingly just" moral victory at 1.2.437–38 ("You taught me language . . .") and "the rich, irreducible concreteness" of 2.2.173–78 ("let me bring thee where crabs grow") that compels us to acknowledge "the independence and integrity of Caliban's construction of reality." In the final scene Prospero acknowledges his moral responsibility for Caliban at 5.1.330–31 ("this thing of darkness I acknowledge mine"), indicating a "deep, if entirely unsentimental," bond between the two; even so, the end of the play leaves Caliban's fate "naggingly unclear": Shakespeare places Caliban "at the outer limits of difference only to insist upon a mysterious measure of resemblance. It is as if he were testing our capacity to sustain metaphor. And in this instance only, the audience achieves a fullness of understanding before Prospero does, an understanding that Prospero is only groping toward at the play's close."

Greenblatt, Stephen. "Martial Law in the Land of Cockaigne." In *Shakespearean Negotiations: The Circulation of Social Energy in Renaissance England*, pp. 129–63 (esp. 142–63). Berkeley: University of California Press, 1988.

Greenblatt examines *The Tempest* in the context of sixteenth-century techniques for exerting control through the production of what was then regarded as a thoroughly salutary anxiety in one's subordinates. He argues that the strategies used by government institutions to arouse and manipulate anxiety in order to fashion the individual subject are "crucial elements in the representational technology of the Elizabethan and Jacobean theater," itself a "virtual machine" for inducing anxiety. Examples of manipulated distress for salutary purposes include Miranda's uneasiness as she watches the conjured storm and shipwreck, the suffering to which Prospero subjects her as he tortures Ferdinand, and the harpy scene in which Prospero torments Antonio, Alonso, Sebastian, and their party. The play's "most memorable yet perplexing moment" (4.1.155–62) comes when "the princely artist puts himself through the paralyzing uneasiness with which he has afflicted others"; suddenly remembering Caliban's "foul conspiracy" against his life, Prospero abruptly breaks off the wedding masque, thereby underscoring his "deep complicity in his present tribulations, for only by actively willing them can he undo the tribulations that he unwillingly and unwittingly brought about years before." For Greenblatt, the interruption of the masque crystallizes the premise on which the entire action of the play rests: namely, "that value lies in controlled uneasiness, and hence that a direct reappropriation of the usurped dukedom and a direct punishment of the usurpers has less moral and political value than an elaborate inward restaging of loss, misery, and anxiety." The distress proves salutary in that from it "reconciliation and pardon . . . issue forth."

But as Antonio's silence when Prospero "forgive[s his] rankest fault" and "require[s his] dukedom" (5.1.149–54) suggests, "the strategy . . . cannot remake the inner life of everyone." Greenblatt extends his discussion of "salutary anxiety" to the play's sources, chiefly William Strachey's account of the shipwrecked *Sea Venture* on its voyage to Jamestown, Virginia in 1609 (see the Alden T. Vaughan and Louis B Wright items below).

Knights, L. C. *"The Tempest."* In *Shakespeare's Late Plays: Essays in Honor of Charles Crow*, edited by Richard C. Tobias and Paul G. Zolbrod, pp. 15–31. Athens: Ohio University Press, 1974.

Knights argues that one must begin one's study of *The Tempest* by recognizing that paradox is its very essence. As a way of "clear[ing] the ground for criticism," he recommends paying attention to four aspects of the play's "surface technique": its conformance to the unities of time and place, its relationship to Jacobean masque, its integral use of music and song, and its wide range of linguistic styles. A key paradox central to a fuller appreciation of the play is Prospero's anger when, during the masque of Ceres, he suddenly recalls "the foul conspiracy" of Caliban, Stephano, and Trinculo (4.1.154 SD–162). Why is he so angry about an insurrection his magic can easily control? The answer lies in both his "special relationship" with Caliban and in his recognition that unlike the masque, life is not so easily controlled: "Caliban, pure instinct, is still plotting; and it is the sudden memory of this that puts Prospero into a 'passion.' . . . No one is put into that kind of temper by external danger . . . , only by self-insurrection." For Knights, the play "is mainly the drama of Prospero, a man who . . . is looking towards the end of his days, trying to sort out and to come to terms with his experiences. Prospero is not simply above the action, controlling it, he is intimately involved. The play is about what Prospero sees, and, above all, what he is and has it in him to become."

Lupton, Julia Reinhard. "The Minority of Caliban." Chapter 6 of *Thinking with Shakespeare: Essays on Politics and Life*, pp. 187–218. Chicago: University of Chicago Press, 2011.

Drawing on the views of the political theorist Hannah Arendt, Lupton reflects on biopolitical moments in Shakespeare "in which . . . political questions come up against problems of life and living." Caliban's status as a minor provides a series of such moments in *The Tempest*. Central to Lupton's reading of the character "in relation to juridical categories of childhood and nonage" is John Locke's *Second Treatise of Government* (published in 1698), a "counter-patriarchal" exploration of paternal duties and filial rights in which "the flow of obligation arises from the right of the child to shelter and education rather than from the absolute sovereignty of the father over his offspring." Locke's "cast of characters"—the single mother, the wild child, and the foster father—and their Shakespeare counterparts—Sycorax, Caliban, and Prospero—lead Lupton to conceptualize Caliban as a minor under Prospero's guardianship, a minor with legal disabilities and privileges. The role of guardian "limits Prospero's sovereignty over Caliban [and makes] Prospero accountable" for failing to protect Caliban's "equality in potentia," i.e., the "unrealized capacity for independence" he bears as a minor. "Arguably Shakespeare's most self-consciously Jacobean play," *The Tempest* reflects on the sovereignty of James I. "Reading Locke's critique of absolutist patriarchalism back into [the] play delivers both a counter-Jacobean Prospero, chastened by his imperfect exercise of paternal duty, as well as a rights-bearing Caliban, whose passage through the disparate conditions of the orphan, the foster child, [the incarcerated juvenile], and the slave ultimately establish his participation in personhood, understood as both a legal category and a subjective possibility." Lupton's Arendtian approach to *The Tempest* by way of Locke moves the discussion of the Prospero-Caliban relationship beyond the prevalent historicist focus on "colonial power and indigenous subjection" into the area of parental responsibilities and children's rights, thereby demonstrating Shakespeare's universality. The minor represents "a particularly potent case of the universal moment that galvanizes progressive and emancipatory movements within plural politics and across global interests": "Perhaps this minor Caliban will reach his majority precisely because he aims for personhood in ways that resonate across authors and interests, continents and centuries." [The chapter incorporates Lupton's earlier essay "The Minority of Caliban: Thinking with Shakespeare and Locke," *REAL: Yearbook of Research in English and American Literature* 22 (2006): 1–35.]

Mowat, Barbara A. "Prospero, Agrippa, and Hocus Pocus." *English Literary Renaissance* 11 (1981): 281–303.
    Mowat argues that Prospero's magic cannot be contained within the "easy dichotomy" of "quintessential Renaissance philosopher-magus" and "potentially damned sorcerer" suggested in much of *The Tempest*'s critical discourse. A close examination of the character's language and actions in the context of several images of magicians available to Shakespeare and his early modern audience—good magus (e.g., occultists like the sixteenth-century Cornelius Agrippa), pagan enchanter, and, perhaps most important, the multi-

faceted wizard who combines elements of the first two with "the Christian's concern over the fate of his soul"— reveals elements of each type, thus making clear "the complexity of [Prospero's] image and of the response which he summons from his audience." For the magus lineage, Mowat cites 1.2.93–95, 109–13, 196–200, and 215–19; for the pagan enchanter, 5.1.50–59; and for the wizard, 5.1.59–66; to all of which she adds the tradition of the "streetcorner 'art-Magician' or 'Jugler'" and his boy apprentice (1.2.281–362). In Prospero we hear echoes of characters as varied as Robert Greene's Friar Bacon, Christopher Marlowe's Dr. Faustus, Shakespeare's Owen Glendower, and the commedia dell'arte's "Pantaloonlet." Prospero is too much of a "wonder . . . himself" to be limited by "magic traditions, black or white.": "[H]owever we view him, the final image which lingers in our minds is of the mortal creature of the epilogue—the magus who has learned to think of his mortality, the Faustus who successfully destroyed his book, the illusionist who stands before us revealing the tricks of his trade." [This article is included in the Virginia and Alden Vaughan collection cited below, pp. 193–213.]

Mowat, Barbara A. "Prospero's Book." *Shakespeare Quarterly* 52 (2001): 1–33.
Along with Prospero's magic robe (5.1.0SD) and magic staff (5.1.60–63), the text of *The Tempest* calls for a book that is the source of his magic (3.1.113–15 and 5.1.66). Puzzled by the "scholarly silence" surrounding this book, Mowat recovers a lost literary tradition—the magic manuscript books used by early modern conjurers such as John Dee—to argue that such books, called "grimoires," lie behind Prospero's book of magic. Mowat's examination of extant grimoires, most notably two late sixteenth-century conjuring books writ-

ten primarily in English—Book 15 of Reginald Scot's *The discouerie of witchcraft* and a manuscript in the Folger Shakespeare Library Collection (catalogued as Folger MS Vb26)—leads her to conclude that the book Prospero uses to summon spirits "both is and is not a grimoire." Like its generic model, Prospero's conjuring book provides him with instructions and materials for calling forth spirits and creating storms (e.g., magic circles, tables, and charts). Unlike the grimoire master's tone, however, which is religious and cautious, Prospero's tone is insouciant and arrogant (4.1.40–42, 4.1.158 and SD), and the types of spirits he summons (see 5.1.42–59) differ radically from those associated with the grimoire (e.g., "Old Testament pagan gods, Christian angels, Cabalistic demons, biblical devils, and Babylonian monsters"). Prospero's creation of spectacle is also "closer to the counterfactual world of fiction than to most grimoires." Mowat claims that "just as Prospero himself is simultaneously (or perhaps alternately) a serious master of spirits and a stage-or-romance wizard who also reminds us . . . of a Renaissance magus and a Jacobean street magician" (see the Mowat item annotated above), his magic book has "multiple counterparts," appearing to be "simultaneously a grimoire and a stage-prop (or romance-prop) grimoire." The final pages of the essay discuss how Prospero's book "can lead to a convergence of magician and explorer / conqueror," thereby linking the study of the grimoire tradition with the current historicist emphasis on the play "as a colonialist document." Several pages of the Folger artifact are reproduced in the article.

Neill, Michael. "*The Tempest*: 'Hush, and be mute': silences in *The Tempest*." In *Late Shakespeare 1608–1613*, edited by Andrew J. Power and Rory Loughnane, pp. 88–107. Cambridge: Cambridge University Press, 2013.

Neill's discussion of Shakespeare's extensive exploitation of "the theatrical effectiveness of silence" in *The Tempest* leads to the assertion that the play's "silences form part of a complex and self-conscious arrangement of acoustic effects unparalleled in early modern theatre." Neill distinguishes between the suspension of all speech and what Philip McGuire calls "open silences," which occur when characters seem to "withdraw into unspeaking privacy, while dialogue continues around them": e.g., Isabella's speechlessness in *Measure for Measure* at the moment the Duke proposes marriage and Antonio's muteness in *The Tempest* when Prospero demands the return of his dukedom. Because it is so difficult to "delimit" the potential significance of such silences, Neill concentrates on what he describes as "closed silences"—those places in the text "where either dialogue, or stage directions, or metrical incompletion are expressly used either to require the silencing of certain characters or to dictate a complete, if temporary, hushing of speech and/or sound." He gives as examples Alonso's and the courtiers' "tongue-tied astonishment" when Ariel in the shape of a harpy denounces the royal party (3.3.109–10, 114–15) and their being agonizingly frozen by Prospero inside his magic circle (5.1.66SD). An example of metrical incompletion prompting momentary silence is Ariel's "I thought to have told thee of it, but I feared / Lest I might anger thee"; the incomplete line suggests a pause by Prospero as he assesses the impact of Ariel's fear before responding, "Say again, where didst thou leave these varlets" (4.1.187–89). Another such metrical example occurs when Gonzalo can be felt mustering his courage in the incomplete "My lord Sebastian," followed by "The truth you speak doth lack some gentleness / And time to speak it in" (2.1.147–49). Prospero's "Hush, and be mute, / Or else our spell is marred" links silence not only to the efficacy of a magician's spells but, as in *The Winter's Tale*, "to the emotions of wonder and amazement that they are calculated to arouse." While sound is crucial to the dramatic meaning of the play (see Neill's "'Noises, / Sounds, and sweet airs': The Burden of Shakespeare's *Tempest*," *Shakespeare Quarterly* 59 [2008]: 36–59), "so too is its absence," as evidenced by the playwright's careful weaving of pauses and episodes of unspeaking "into the fabric of the composition."

Orgel, Stephen. *The Illusion of Power: Political Theatre in the English Renaissance.* Berkeley: University of California Press, 1975.

Orgel's book consists of three chapters: "Theaters and Audiences," "The Royal Spectacle," and "The Role of King"; he discusses *The Tempest* in chapter 2 (pp. 37–58, esp. pp. 44–49), focusing specifically on the conjured entertainment involving the goddesses Ceres, Juno, and Iris (4.1.66SD–158SD). In this royal masque, which is also a wedding masque, Shakespeare provides an "essay on the power and art of the royal imagination," masques serving as "the expression of the monarch's will, the mirrors of his mind." As Orgel notes, Prospero's spectacle is not a real masque "but a dramatic representation of one, . . . unique in that its creator is also the monarch at its center." In the otherwise tight temporal control of *The Tempest*, where the action's time span corresponds exactly to the play's performance time, the masque has its own temporal scheme as it moves through the seasons from spring through summer and harvest and then back to spring, skipping winter in a pointed emphasis on the wonders and growth of nature. What brings the masque to an abrupt end is not the arrival of winter but the threat of

death posed by Caliban's conspiracy. Prospero's awareness of time—as it "comprehends both the masque and
the drama"—is both "his art and his power, producing
on the one hand his sense of the world as an insubstantial pageant [4.1.172], and on the other, his total
command of the action moment by moment." Imagination here is real power, and "the source of the power
is imagination," an active and outgoing faculty in Prospero, whose power links him to Renaissance ideas of
both gods and kings.

Patrick, Julian. "*The Tempest* as Supplement." In *Centre
and Labyrinth: Essays in Honour of Northrop Frye*, pp.
162–80. Toronto: University of Toronto Press, 1983.
    Patrick associates *The Tempest* with "the middle
stages of romance," which "are both unstable and
actively generative." He identifies such instability as
arising from the play of past, present, and future in the
form of the characters' narratives, actions, and goals,
in all of which the audience is involved. The close relationship between the audience and the extraordinary
spectacles produced only to dissolve (e.g., the beginning shipwreck and the masque of Ceres) is empha-
sized by the fact that the events are unfolding in the
same time period for the characters on stage as for the
audience watching in the theater. Because the tempest
that opens the play happens in front of us without any
mediating preparatory event, "it is as if we were being
hurried right into the centre of time itself as we see a
whole society, from King to sailor, apparently being
destroyed." Patrick examines Miranda's response to the
shipwreck (1.2.1–13) as a way of gaining some understanding both of the play's "haunting and tantalizing
picture of human time" and of the paradoxical position
of the audience of *The Tempest*, linked by time to the
onstage events but displaced and marginalized by the

motive and direction of events that move "from nature to art and from action to contemplation." For Patrick, from 1.2 until almost the very end, "what happens on stage happens to other audiences than us, as we watch others being watched." Something changes, however, in the epilogue when the audience is asked to fill the ship's sails and speed it back to Naples. Because of the seriousness with which the epilogue insists that only the audience can save Prospero from despair, it "is not a mere supplement to [*The Tempest*] but its necessary conclusion," suddenly revealing the audience "to be, not the marginal and displaced onlooker of the play but the implied subject, its judge and, in a way, its creator." The play's real closure, then, "lies in the imaginative capacity and commitment of the theatre-audience."

Skura, Meredith. "Discourse and the Individual: The Case of Colonialism in *The Tempest*." *Shakespeare Quarterly* 40 (1989): 42–69.

In explicit reaction to interpretations of *The Tempest* as implicated in colonial discourse, Skura offers readings of the play that link it instead to other types of discourse, the chief one being the Shakespeare canon, which provides many precursors of Prospero and Caliban (e.g., Prince Hal and Falstaff [*Henry IV, Parts 1* and *2*], Duke Senior and Jacques [*As You Like It*], and Duke Vincentio and Lucio [*Measure for Measure*]). She argues that the New Historicist approach to the play "flattens the text into the mold of colonialist discourse and eliminates what is characteristically Shakespearean in order to foreground what is 'colonialist.'" Claiming that the play "insists" that we view Prospero's current relation to Caliban in terms of "the framing story of [Prospero's] own family history" and that "childishness" is essential to defining Caliban, Skura applies traditional psychological models to an analysis of the parent-child relationship informing the Prospero-Caliban dynamic, for which she finds a key precedent in *Titus Andronicus*'s Aaron the Moor and the "childish thing of darkness" he fathers. Skura's "conjunction of the psychological and the political" encourages a "recognition of the individuality of the play, and of Shakespeare, [that] does not counter but rather enriches the understanding of [the historical] context": "What the example of Caliban's childish presence in the play suggests is that for Shakespeare the desire for . . . utopias has roots in personal history as well as in 'history.'" [The essay is included in the Virginia and Alden Vaughan collection cited below, pp. 60–90.]

Vaughan, Alden. "William Strachey's 'True Reportory' and Shakespeare: a closer look at the evidence." *Shakespeare Quarterly* 59 (2008): 245–73.

In this study of one of *The Tempest*'s generally accepted sources, one with significant implications for determining the play's date of origin, Vaughan joins the debate concerning the relation of William Strachey's letter "A True Reportory" to Shakespeare's play. Addressed to an anonymous "Excellent Lady" living in England, Strachey's eyewitness account of the *Sea Venture*, shipwrecked in July 1609 while en route to Jamestown, Virginia, describes the storm that befell the ship, the amazing survival of passengers and crew, the castaways' "remarkable interlude on Bermuda" (where the ship foundered), the voyagers' final arrival in Jamestown, and the deplorable state of affairs found there. After a careful review of the context and content of the letter, Vaughan turns to a point-by-point rebuttal of modern challenges to the standard thesis that "A True Reportory" played a formative role in the composition of the play. The author's research into the trajectory of the letter from Jamestown to London in the fall of 1610, where it circulated in manuscript among officials of the Virginia Company of London, which had promoted the colonizing expedition, leads him to conclude that Strachey's narrative was available to Shakespeare, who personally knew several of the company officials, one of whom was his patron the earl of Southampton. In the final part of the article, Vaughan addresses specific verbal and thematic similarities between the letter and the play to demonstrate that while Shakespeare drew on other sources in composing *The Tempest*, "Strachey offered a basic outline for the play's meteorological and insular elements and for many of its human interactions." The article is illustrated with maps from the time and details from Strachey's letter as it first appeared in print in 1625. For an edition of the letter, see Wright, below.

Vaughan, Alden T., and Virginia Mason Vaughan. *Shakespeare's Caliban: A Cultural History*. Cambridge: Cambridge University Press, 1991.

In this interdisciplinary investigation of the protean afterlife of Shakespeare's Caliban, the Vaughans begin with his "debut" in the 1623 Folio text; they then turn to the historical and literary contexts surrounding his genesis. Among the former are documents relating to Europe's "discovery" of the Western Hemisphere, "the prevailing image of Indians" in the iconography of the sixteenth and early seventeenth centuries, Montaigne's essay "Of the Caniballes," and accounts of the sociopolitical world of Jacobean England. Caliban's literary contexts include monsters from medieval and early modern romances, figures from commedia dell'arte and antimasques, and, most importantly, the wild man of popular folklore, civic pageantry, and sixteenth-century poetry and drama, a figure with roots in such classical texts as Homer's *Odyssey*, Virgil's *Aeneid*, and Ovid's *Metamorphoses*. "Part III: Receptions" is the heart of the book; here, the authors trace Caliban's odyssey through three and a half centuries across a variety of media: critical discourse, theatrical and cinematic productions, renditions in visual art, and poetic invocations. The many critical interpretations of Caliban (e.g., as "quasi-human monster," American Indian, and the indigenous victim of imperialist oppression), coupled with myriad imaginative depictions (e.g., as amphibian, punk rocker, and black militant), "attest to the [character's] integral place in our cultural heritage," establishing Shakespeare's creation as a "cultural signifier" open to endless transformations "yet . . . always recognizable." In the final chapter, which looks to the future, the Vaughans predict a continuation of the "softening of the binary opposition between Prospero the master and Caliban the slave" that began in the 1950s. Caliban's odyssey "promises to . . . remain 'rich and strange,' for, paradoxically, Caliban is simultaneously one of Shakespeare's most ambiguous and most memorable characters."

Vaughan, Virginia Mason, and Alden T. Vaughan, eds. *Critical Essays on Shakespeare's "The Tempest."* New York: G. K. Hall, 1998.

This collection of ten essays covers sources and analogues in classical literature and mythology, colonial and dynastic politics, performance history, critical readings, and political and social appropriations of the play. The essays are as follows: Donna B. Hamilton's "Defiguring Virgil in *The Tempest*," Jonathan Bate's "From Myth to Drama," Meredith Anne Skura's "The Case of Colonialism in *The Tempest*" (see annotation above), David Scott Kastan's "'The Duke of Milan / And His Brave Son': Dynastic Politics in *The Tempest*,"

Keith Sturgess's "'A Quaint Device': *The Tempest* at the Blackfriars," Trevor R. Griffith's "'This Island's Mine': Caliban and Colonialism" (an examination of the effects of colonialism and slavery on stage renditions in the nineteenth century), Roger Warren's "Rough Magic and Heavenly Music: *The Tempest*" (an analysis of Peter Hall's 1988 National Theatre production), Barbara A. Mowat's "Prospero, Agrippa, and Hocus Pocus" (see annotation above), Russ McDonald's "Reading *The Tempest*," Ann Thompson's "'Miranda, Where's Your Sister?': Reading Shakespeare's *The Tempest*," and Alden T. Vaughan's "Caliban in the 'Third World': Shakespeare's Savage as Sociopolitical Symbol." In their introductory essay "*The Tempest* Transformed," the Vaughans address the history of the play's reception from the 1667 Dryden-Davenant adaptation *The Tempest: or, The Enchanted Island* (which "nearly monopolized" the stage until William Charles Macready restored the original text in 1838) through the dual lenses of nineteenth-century romanticism and Darwinian evolutionary theory to the "Americanization [of the play] that dominated interpretive trends through most of the twentieth century." This last approach eventually gave way, on one hand, to the colonialist—"or, more accurately, anticolonialist"—readings of New Historicists in the 1970s and 1980s and, on the other, to a widening view of *The Tempest* as not "simply an Anglo-American play." Understood as a series of "intersecting journeys, transformations, interpretive confrontations, and uncertainties," the history of the play's complex critical and performance afterlife promises to "keep . . . moving in unpredictable but provocative and pleasurable directions." As evidence for this claim, the editors point to recent appropriations by African and Caribbean postcolonial writers, feminist poets and novelists, and "avant-garde" filmmakers (namely, Derek Jarman, Paul Mazursky, and Peter Greenaway).

Wright, Louis B., ed. *A Voyage to Virginia in 1609: Two Narratives.* Charlottesville: University Press of Virginia, 1964.

Wright here edits two early seventeenth-century narratives describing the 1609 wreck off the Bermuda Islands of the *Sea Venture* (the flagship of a nine vessel flotilla headed for Jamestown, Virginia) and the miraculous saving of the new governor of Virginia, the admiral of the fleet, and all of the ship's passengers and crew. The accounts are William Strachey's letter to an unnamed lady, titled "A True Reportory of the Wreck and Redemption of Sir Thomas Gates, Knight, upon and from the Islands of the Bermudas: His Coming to Virginia and the Estate of that Colony Then and After, under the Government of the Lord La Warr, July 15, 1610," and Sylvester Jourdain's "A Discovery of the Bermudas, Otherwise Called the Isle of Devils." The former, having reached England in the fall of 1610, circulated in manuscript before being printed in 1625 as part of Samuel Purchas's *Purchas His Pilgrimes*, an extensive collection of travel literature. Jourdain's narrative was printed in London in 1610, thus making it the first published record of the disaster and its aftermath. Both have long been considered sources of Shakespeare's *The Tempest*. In his introduction (pp. ix–xx), Wright provides a succinct account of the voyage and its relation to Shakespeare's play; he also includes biographical details pertaining to Strachey and Jourdain. Besides being of interest to Shakespeareans, the narratives "are both intrinsically fascinating documents and have a significant place in the voyage literature of their day." They are reprinted here for the first time with the spelling, punctuation, and capitalization modernized. (For more on "True Reportory," see Alden Vaughan's article annotated above.)

Shakespeare's Language

Abbott, E. A. *A Shakespearian Grammar.* New York: Haskell House, 1972.

This compact reference book, first published in 1870, helps with many difficulties in Shakespeare's language. It systematically accounts for a host of differences between Shakespeare's usage and sentence structure and our own.

Blake, Norman. *Shakespeare's Language: An Introduction.* New York: St. Martin's Press, 1983.

This general introduction to Elizabethan English discusses various aspects of the language of Shakespeare and his contemporaries, offering possible meanings for hundreds of ambiguous constructions.

Dobson, E. J. *English Pronunciation, 1500–1700.* 2 vols. Oxford: Clarendon Press, 1968.

This long and technical work includes chapters on spelling (and its reformation), phonetics, stressed vowels, and consonants in early modern English.

Hope, Jonathan. *Shakespeare's Grammar.* London: Arden Shakespeare, 2003.

Commissioned as a replacement for Abbott's *Shakespearian Grammar*, Hope's book is organized in terms of the two basic parts of speech, the noun and the verb. After extensive analysis of the noun phrase and the verb phrase come briefer discussions of subjects and agents, objects, complements, and adverbials.

Houston, John. *Shakespearean Sentences: A Study in Style and Syntax.* Baton Rouge: Louisiana State University Press, 1988.

Houston studies Shakespeare's stylistic choices, considering matters such as sentence length and the relative positions of subject, verb, and direct object. Examining plays throughout the canon in a roughly chronological, developmental order, he analyzes how sentence structure is used in setting tone, in characterization, and for other dramatic purposes.

Onions, C. T. *A Shakespeare Glossary.* Oxford: Clarendon Press, 1986.

This revised edition updates Onions's standard, selective glossary of words and phrases in Shakespeare's plays that are now obsolete, archaic, or obscure.

Robinson, Randal. *Unlocking Shakespeare's Language: Help for the Teacher and Student.* Urbana, Ill.: National Council of Teachers of English and the ERIC Clearinghouse on Reading and Communication Skills, 1989.

Specifically designed for the high-school and undergraduate college teacher and student, Robinson's book addresses the problems that most often hinder present-day readers of Shakespeare. Through work with his own students, Robinson found that many readers today are particularly puzzled by such stylistic characteristics as subject-verb inversion, interrupted structures, and compression. He shows how our own colloquial language contains comparable structures, and thus helps students recognize such structures when they find them in Shakespeare's plays. This book supplies worksheets—with examples from major plays—to illuminate and remedy such problems as unusual sequences of words and the separation of related parts of sentences.

Williams, Gordon. *A Dictionary of Sexual Language and Imagery in Shakespearean and Stuart Literature*. 3 vols. London: Athlone Press, 1994.
    Williams provides a comprehensive list of words to which Shakespeare, his contemporaries, and later Stuart writers gave sexual meanings. He supports his identification of these meanings by extensive quotations.

Shakespeare's Life

Baldwin, T. W. *William Shakspere's Petty School*. Urbana: University of Illinois Press, 1943.
    Baldwin here investigates the theory and practice of the petty school, the first level of education in Elizabethan England. He focuses on that educational system primarily as it is reflected in Shakespeare's art.

Baldwin, T. W. *William Shakspere's Small Latine and Lesse Greeke*. 2 vols. Urbana: University of Illinois Press, 1944.
    Baldwin attacks the view that Shakespeare was an uneducated genius—a view that had been dominant among Shakespeareans since the eighteenth century. Instead, Baldwin shows, the educational system of Shakespeare's time would have given the playwright a strong background in the classics, and there is much in the plays that shows how Shakespeare benefited from such an education.

Beier, A. L., and Roger Finlay, eds. *London 1500–1700: The Making of the Metropolis*. New York: Longman, 1986.

Focusing on the economic and social history of early modern London, these collected essays probe aspects of metropolitan life, including "Population and Disease," "Commerce and Manufacture," and "Society and Change."

Chambers, E. K. *William Shakespeare: A Study of Facts and Problems*. 2 vols. Oxford: Clarendon Press, 1930.
Analyzing in great detail the scant historical data, Chambers's complex, scholarly study considers the nature of the texts in which Shakespeare's work is preserved.

Cressy, David. *Education in Tudor and Stuart England*. London: Edward Arnold, 1975.
This volume collects sixteenth-, seventeenth-, and early eighteenth-century documents detailing aspects of formal education in England, such as the curriculum, the control and organization of education, and the education of women.

Duncan-Jones, Katherine. *Shakespeare: An Ungentle Life*. London: Arden Shakespeare, 2010.
This biography, first published in 2001 under the title *Ungentle Shakespeare: Scenes from His Life*, sets out to look into the documents from Shakespeare's personal life—especially legal and financial records—and it finds there a man very different from the one portrayed in more traditional biographies. He is "ungentle" in being born to a lower social class and in being a bit ruthless and more than a bit stingy. As the author notes, "three topics were formerly taboo both in polite society and in Shakespearean biography: social class, sex and money. I have been indelicate enough to give a good deal of attention to all three." She examines "Shakespeare's uphill struggle to achieve, or purchase, 'gentle' status."

She finds that "Shakespeare was strongly interested in intense relationships with well-born young men." And she shows that he was "reluctant to divert much, if any, of his considerable wealth towards charitable, neighbourly, or altruistic ends." She insists that his plays and poems are "great, and enduring," and that it is in them "that the best of him is to be found."

Dutton, Richard. *William Shakespeare: A Literary Life*. New York: St. Martin's Press, 1989.

Not a biography in the traditional sense, Dutton's very readable work nevertheless "follows the contours of Shakespeare's life" as it examines Shakespeare's career as playwright and poet, with consideration of his patrons, theatrical associations, and audience.

Honan, Park. *Shakespeare: A Life*. New York: Oxford University Press, 1998.

Honan's accessible biography focuses on the various contexts of Shakespeare's life—physical, social, political, and cultural—to place the dramatist within a lucidly described world. The biography includes detailed examinations of, for example, Stratford schooling, theatrical politics of 1590s London, and the careers of Shakespeare's associates. The author draws on a wealth of established knowledge and on interesting new research into local records and documents; he also engages in speculation about, for example, the possibilities that Shakespeare was a tutor in a Catholic household in the north of England in the 1580s and that he acted particular roles in his own plays, areas that reflect new, but unproven and debatable, data—though Honan is usually careful to note where a particular narrative "has not been capable of proof or disproof."

Potter, Lois. *The Life of William Shakespeare: A Critical Biography*. Malden, Mass.: Wiley-Blackwell, 2012.

This critical biography of Shakespeare takes the playwright from cradle to grave, paying primary attention to his literary and theatrical milieu. The chapters "follow a chronological sequence," each focusing on a handful of years in the playwright's life. In the chapters that cover his playwriting years (5–17), each chapter focuses on events in Stratford-upon-Avon and in London (especially in the commercial theaters) while giving equal space to discussions of the plays and/or poems Shakespeare wrote during those years. Filled with information from Shakespeare's literary and theatrical worlds, the biography also shares frequent insights into how modern productions of a given play can shed light on the play, especially in scenes that Shakespeare's text presents ambiguously.

Schoenbaum, S. *William Shakespeare: A Compact Documentary Life*. New York: Oxford University Press, 1977.

Schoenbaum's evidence-based biography of Shakespeare is a compact version of his magisterial folio-size *Shakespeare: A Documentary Life* (New York: Oxford University Press, 1975). Schoenbaum structures his readable "compact" narrative around the documents that still exist which chronicle Shakespeare's familial, theatrical, legal, and financial existence. These documents, along with those discovered since the 1970s, form the basis of almost all Shakespeare biographies written since Schoenbaum's books appeared.

Shakespeare's Theater

Bentley, G. E. *The Profession of Player in Shakespeare's Time, 1590–1642*. Princeton: Princeton University Press, 1984.

Bentley readably sets forth a wealth of evidence about performance in Shakespeare's time, with special attention to the relations between player and company, and the business of casting, managing, and touring.

Berry, Herbert. *Shakespeare's Playhouses*. New York: AMS Press, 1987.

Berry's six essays collected here discuss (with illustrations) varying aspects of the four playhouses in which Shakespeare had a financial stake: the Theatre in Shoreditch, the Blackfriars, and the first and second Globe.

Berry, Herbert, William Ingram, and Glynne Wickham, eds. *English Professional Theatre, 1530–1660*. Cambridge: Cambridge University Press, 2000.

Wickham presents the government documents designed to control professional players, their plays, and playing places. Ingram handles the professional actors, giving as representative a life of the actor Augustine Phillips, and discussing, among other topics, patrons, acting companies, costumes, props, playbooks, provincial playing, and child actors. Berry treats the twenty-three different London playhouses from 1560 to 1660 for which there are records, including four inns.

Cook, Ann Jennalie. *The Privileged Playgoers of Shakespeare's London*. Princeton: Princeton University Press, 1981.

Cook's work argues, on the basis of sociological, economic, and documentary evidence, that Shakespeare's audience—and the audience for English Renaissance drama generally—consisted mainly of the "privileged."

Dutton, Richard, ed. *The Oxford Handbook of Early Modern Theatre*. Oxford: Oxford University Press, 2011.

Dutton divides his study of the theatrical industry of Shakespeare's time into the following sections: "Theatre Companies," "London Playhouses," "Other Playing Spaces," "Social Practices," and "Evidence of Theatrical Practices." Each of these sections is further subdivided, with subdivisions assigned to individual experts. W. R. Streitberger treats the "Adult Playing Companies to 1583"; Sally-Beth MacLean those from 1583 to 1593; Roslyn L. Knutson, 1593–1603; Tom Rutter, 1603–1613; James J. Marino, 1613–1625; and Martin Butler, the "Adult and Boy Playing Companies 1625–1642." Michael Shapiro is responsible for the "Early (Pre-1590) Boy Companies and Their Acting Venues," while Mary Bly writes of "The Boy Companies 1599–1613." David Kathman handles "Inn-Yard Playhouses"; Gabriel Egan, "The Theatre in Shoreditch 1576–1599"; Andrew Gurr, "Why the Globe Is Famous"; Ralph Alan Cohen, "The Most Convenient Place: The Second Blackfriars Theater and Its Appeal"; Mark Bayer, "The Red Bull Playhouse"; and Frances Teague, "The Phoenix and the Cockpit-in-Court Playhouses." Turning to "Other Playing Spaces," Suzanne Westfall describes how "'He who pays the piper calls the tune': Household Entertainments"; Alan H. Nelson, "The Universities and the Inns of Court"; Peter Greenfield, "Touring"; John H. Astington, "Court Theatre"; and Anne Lancashire, "London Street Theater." For "Social Practices," Alan Somerset writes of "Not Just Sir Oliver

Owlet: From Patrons to 'Patronage' of Early Modern Theatre," Dutton himself of "The Court, the Master of the Revels, and the Players," S. P. Cerasano of "Theater Entrepreneurs and Theatrical Economics," Ian W. Archer of "The City of London and the Theatre," David Kathman of "Players, Livery Companies, and Apprentices," Kathleen E. McLuskie of "Materiality and the Market: The Lady Elizabeth's Men and the Challenge of Theatre History," Heather Hirschfield of "For the author's credit': Issues of Authorship in English Renaissance Drama," and Natasha Korda of "Women in the Theater." On "Theatrical Practices," Jacalyn Royce discusses "Early Modern Naturalistic Acting: The Role of the Globe in the Development of Personation"; Tiffany Stern, "Actors' Parts"; Alan Dessen, "Stage Directions and the Theater Historian"; R. B. Graves, "Lighting"; Lucy Munro, "Music and Sound"; Dutton himself, "Properties"; Thomas Postlewait, "Eyewitnesses to History: Visual Evidence for Theater in Early Modern England"; and Eva Griffith, "Christopher Beeston: His Property and Properties."

Greg, W. W. *Dramatic Documents from the Elizabethan Playhouses.* 2 vols. Oxford: Clarendon Press, 1931.

Greg itemizes and briefly describes almost all the play manuscripts that survive from the period 1590 to around 1660, including, among other things, players' parts. His second volume offers facsimiles of selected manuscripts.

Harbage, Alfred. *Shakespeare's Audience.* New York: Columbia University Press, 1941.

Harbage investigates the fragmentary surviving evidence to interpret the size, composition, and behavior of Shakespeare's audience.

Keenan, Siobhan. *Acting Companies and Their Plays in Shakespeare's London*. London: Bloomsbury Arden Shakespeare, 2014.

Keenan "explores how the needs, practices, resources and pressures on acting companies and playwrights informed not only the performance and publication of contemporary dramas but playwrights' writing practices." Each chapter focuses on one important factor that influenced Renaissance playwrights and players. The initial focus is on how "the nature and composition of the acting companies" influenced the playwrights who wrote for them. Then, using "the Diary of theatre manager Philip Henslowe and manuscript playbooks showing signs of theatrical use," Keenan examines the relations between acting companies and playwrights. Other influences include "the physical design and facilities of London's outdoor and indoor theatrical spaces" and the diverse audiences for plays, including royal and noble patrons.

Shapiro, Michael. *Children of the Revels: The Boy Companies of Shakespeare's Time and Their Plays*. New York: Columbia University Press, 1977.

Shapiro chronicles the history of the amateur and quasi-professional child companies that flourished in London at the end of Elizabeth's reign and the beginning of James's.

The Publication of Shakespeare's Plays

Blayney, Peter W. M. *The First Folio of Shakespeare*. Hanover, Md.: Folger, 1991.

Blayney's accessible account of the printing and later life of the First Folio—an amply illustrated catalogue to a 1991 Folger Shakespeare Library exhibition—analyzes the mechanical production of the First Folio, describing how the Folio was made, by whom and for whom, how much it cost, and its ups and downs (or, rather, downs and ups) since its printing in 1623.

Hinman, Charlton. *The Norton Facsimile: The First Folio of Shakespeare.* 2nd ed. New York: W. W. Norton, 1996.

This facsimile presents a photographic reproduction of an "ideal" copy of the First Folio of Shakespeare; Hinman attempts to represent each page in its most fully corrected state. This second edition includes an important new introduction by Peter W. M. Blayney.

Hinman, Charlton. *The Printing and Proof-Reading of the First Folio of Shakespeare.* 2 vols. Oxford: Clarendon Press, 1963.

In the most arduous study of a single book ever undertaken, Hinman attempts to reconstruct how the Shakespeare First Folio of 1623 was set into type and run off the press, sheet by sheet. He also provides almost all the known variations in readings from copy to copy.

Werstine, Paul. *Early Modern Playhouse Manuscripts and the Editing of Shakespeare.* Cambridge: Cambridge University Press, 2012.

Werstine examines in detail nearly two dozen texts associated with the playhouses in and around Shakespeare's time, conducting the examination against the background of the two idealized forms of manuscript that have governed the editing of Shakespeare from the twentieth into the twenty-first century—Shakespeare's so-called foul papers and the so-called promptbooks of his plays. By comparing the two extant texts of John Fletcher's *Bonduca*, one in manuscript and the other printed in 1647, Werstine shows that the term "foul papers" that is found in a note in the *Bonduca* manuscript does not refer, as editors have believed, to a species of messy authorial manuscript but is instead simply a designation for a manuscript, whatever its features, that has served as the copy from which another manuscript has been made. By surveying twenty-one texts with theatrical markup, he demonstrates that the playhouses used a wide variety of different kinds of manuscripts and printed texts but did not use the highly regularized promptbooks of the eighteenth-century theaters and later. His presentation of the peculiarities of playhouse texts provides an empirical basis for inferring the nature of the manuscripts that lie behind printed Shakespeare plays.

Key to
Famous Lines and Phrases

Methinks he hath no drowning mark upon him. His
complexion is perfect gallows.
[*Gonzalo*—1.1.29–31]

In the dark backward and abysm of time.
[*Prospero*—1.2.62]

... the still-vexed Bermoothes ...   [*Ariel*—1.2.272]

You taught me language, and my profit on 't
Is I know how to curse.   [*Caliban*—1.2.437–38]

Song. Come unto these yellow sands ...
[*Ariel*—1.2.452–64]

Song. Full fathom five thy father lies ...
[*Ariel*—1.2.474–82]

There's nothing ill can dwell in such a temple.
If the ill spirit have so fair a house,
Good things will strive to dwell with 't.
[*Miranda*—1.2.552–54]

He receives comfort like cold porridge.
[*Sebastian*—2.1.11–12]

... what's past is prologue ...   [*Antonio*—2.1.289]

They'll take suggestion as a cat laps milk.
[*Antonio*—2.1.329]

Misery acquaints a man with strange bedfellows.
[*Trinculo*—2.2.40–41]

. . . keep a good tongue in your head.
[*Stephano*—3.2.38]

The isle is full of noises,
Sounds and sweet airs that give delight and hurt not.
[*Caliban*—3.2.148–49]

Our revels now are ended. These our actors,
As I foretold you, were all spirits and
Are melted into air, into thin air . . .
We are such stuff
As dreams are made on, and our little life
Is rounded with a sleep. [*Prospero*—4.1.165–75]

You elves of hills, brooks, standing lakes, and
groves . . . [*Prospero*—5.1.42]

And deeper than did ever plummet sound
I'll drown my book. [*Prospero*—5.1.65–66]

Song. Where the bee sucks, there suck I.
[*Ariel*—5.1.98–104]

How many goodly creatures are there here!
How beauteous mankind is! O, brave new world
That has such people in 't! [*Miranda*—5.1.216–18]

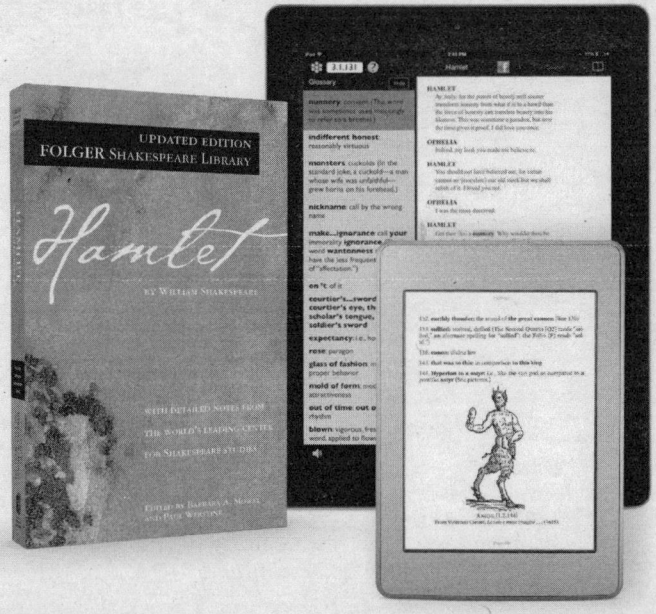